GOD IN THE PHILOSOPHY OF SCHELLING

A DISSERTATION

IN PHILOSOPHY

PRESENTED TO THE FACULTY OF THE GRADUATE SCHOOL OF THE
UNIVERSITY OF PENNSYLVANIA IN PARTIAL FULFILLMENT
OF THE REQUIREMENTS FOR THE DEGREE
OF DOCTOR OF PHILOSOPHY

ROWLAND GRAY-SMITH

PHILADELPHIA

1933

TABLE OF CONTENTS

APPENDIX

Supplement to Jost's Bibliography

MAIN SOURCES OF REFERENCE

"W"

Friedrich Wilhelm Joseph von Schellings sämmtliche
Werke (Stuttgart and Augsburg) 1856

"L"

Aus Schellings Leben in Briefen.
G. L. Plitt (Leipzig) 1869

I

The Absolute I

(*Tübingen, 1790-1795*)

Having closed a brilliant academic career at Tübingen, Schelling returned home and supplied in his father's pulpit some Sundays during the summer of seventeen ninety-five. Though but twenty he had received his Master's degree three years earlier and had spent the remainder of his time at the university qualifying in Theology. Hegel had left Tübingen two years before Schelling and in an exchange of letters we catch a glimpse of the questions that occupied them. Asked for his opinion of the argument for a personal God in connection with the Unconditional of Kant's Ethics, Schelling replied, "We are done with the orthodox conceptions of God. We go farther than the idea of a personal Being"; and thereupon he gave the conclusion to which he had then come: "God is only the Absolute I" (L. I, 77). It is with this conception of God, as contained in the works written by Schelling in his minority, that this chapter is occupied.

The so-called "moral arguments for the existence of God" to which the correspondence referred had widespread popularity among contemporary theologians (W. I, 1, 283). Schelling found himself in wholehearted revolt against the misuse of philosophy on the part of the theologians. While still an undergraduate in Arts he had written his objections against those who, in the crisis in which theology found itself, confronted now with the historical method of the interpretation of the Bible, attempted to avoid, by philosophical subtlety, the purely historical method, and he likens philosophy so used to a wolf in sheep's clothing, a disguised enemy of genuine theology (L. I, 39-40). Having now finished his thesis for graduation in Theology, he sends it to Hegel with the comment that his first thought had been to write upon "the extraordinary weapons of the orthodox of former times against heretics" (L. I, 79).

The weapon of the contemporary orthodox was the Kantian philosophy, and their "moral argument" presented God as an "absolute Object," external to the thinking subject. In the phrase "the absolute I" we have the conception upon which Schelling sharpens his own weapons against them. In contrast to the Theologians, who perverted the philosophy they professed to embrace, Schelling accepts himself as the genuine successor of Kant, and his own Idealism as the inevitable outcome of Criticism. He offers us no calm critical examination of the writings of Kant, but everywhere his brilliant effusions pillory such "Kantians" as he found offering him instruction at the university.

A glance at the reasoning employed by Schelling in his enquiry into the possibility of finding for philosophy a universal Form (1794) will give some intelligibility to the phrase "the absolute I." Kant's Critique of Pure Reason was found lacking in that all the forms in which the mind conceives objects were not led back to one final principle (W. I, 1, 88). Without such a final principle philosophizing is impossible, and he is thankful to Fichte for pleasantly surprising him with a new writing (On the Theory of Knowledge) that makes his own task the easier. The "I" is the experiencing subject, and in opposition to it is set the "not-I," in which term is bundled together the manifold objects present to the mind of the experiencing subject. Since the "I" and the "not-I" stand in mutual relation, the "I" conditioned by the "not-I" and conversely, neither is absolute; neither, therefore, is good enough to serve as the absolutely unconditioned principle that philosophy must have (W. I, 1, 92). It is necessary to emphasize that Schelling does not proceed to make the relativity of the subject and object into the absolute principle; nor does he make "selfconsciousness" that principle (so Watson's *Schelling's Transcendental Idealism*, p. 71). On the contrary he distinguishes it from selfconsciousness (W. I, 1, 100; 180; 200; 324). What Schelling does is to pass from the bad predicament of two relatives and to set up an "absolute I" which has absolute causality in itself and which is a pre-condition both of the "I" and "not-I." From the standpoint of this "absolute I" he attacks, among others, the contemporary theologians, the century-old Spinozism, and the post-Kantian Reinhold. These three will provide us with a three-fold account of how the "absolute I" is *not* to be taken.

The theologians were quick to seize upon both the weakness of human reason as presented in Kant's mental philosophy and the necessity of faith in God as presented in his moral philosophy. Schelling's criticisms are penetrating. While happiness is excluded from the imperative of morality, it is postulated that happiness shall be combined with morality (W. I, 1, 201). Introducing God merely as a moral postulate, they pass to the anthropomorphic idea of God as a moral Being. Glorifying in the weakness of speculative reason, with its inability to know anything about the "thing-in-itself," and admitting the impossibility of establishing an absolute causality, they deify the "thing-in-itself" (Cf. W. I, 1, 358) and introduce on moral grounds affirmations forbidden on rational grounds. Such is the *Deus ex machina* of those who tune down philosophy to preachers' litanies (W. I, 1, 288-9). He nowhere suggests that Kant himself was open to such criticism, and ten years later, in a foreword to a new edition, declares that none of those who had remained at the standpoint attacked had answered him (W. I, 1, 283).

There can be no absolute "He." "Let us posit God as object and assume him to be the real ground of our knowledge. Then, as an object, he falls within the sphere of our knowledge. Thus, being within the sphere of our knowledge, he cannot be that upon which the whole sphere depends" (W. I, 1, 165). "Believing in an absolute Object means that I, as a believing subject, have already ceased to exist" (Ib. 287-8). "Before you believe in an objective God, his causality has negated yours" (Ib. 290). "There is no God as object, but merely pure, absolute I" (Ib. 202). "Since the object is a representation in the mind of man, since man gives the object its form and conditions, man rules it. He has nothing to fear from it; he himself sets its limits. If he abolishes these limits, if the object can no longer be represented in his mind, he finds himself lost" (Ib. 337).

The condemnation of Theology as "Dogmatism," because it postulated an absolute Object, stretches also to Spinoza, his respect for whom is in marked contrast to his contempt for the theologians. His comparison strikes an aesthetic note. The aesthetic appeal of the logical dogmatism of Spinoza, the "quiet intuition of rest in the arms of the world in the highest moment of life" is absent from the moral dogmatism of the theologians (W. I, 1, 284-5). Yet when Spinoza required the identity of the subjective causality with the objective causality he attested that the finite causality is only a modification of the infinite causality, and annulled that which makes the I, I, its independent causality (Ib. 316). "Spinoza has set up as the first principle of all philosophy a proposition that could only be set up at the end of his system as the result of the most painstaking proof" (Ib. 309). In fact, what Spinoza has done is to represent as an absolute Object what is only an intuition of his "I," and the content of his Absolute is but the projection to the outside of the self of what he has borrowed from self-intuition (Ib. 317-321). For Schelling, however, "everything that is, is in the I, and outside of it is nothing" (Ib. 192). "I have become a Spinozist," and his "Spinozism" displaces with the "absolute I," the "World," the "absolute Object," the "absolute not-I" that Spinoza required as the foundation of his philosophy (L. I, 76).

From the definition of the "absolute I" we have so far excluded two possibilities. It is neither the absolute "He" nor the absolute "It"; he is thinking neither theistically nor pantheistically. The negative definition is complete when we add that neither is the "absolute I" any kind of consciousness. Reinhold's attempt to make Kant's philosophy a monism was the morning light that precedes the noon-day (L. I, 75) and worthy of the highest respect (W. I, 1, 175). The Kantian analyses of the mind's capacities are put together in the one capacity, the unity of consciousness. Can, then, consciousness be a mediator between subject and object? Above the mutual relation of subject to object there is a relation of both to consciousness. But Reinhold's merit is only to present the question in a higher abstraction and so to prepare the way for a sure answer (Ib. 176), for that which is, indeed, higher than all abstraction. The "I think" turns out to be "I think about . . ."; it does not exist through its mere existence; "it is an expression, not of an absolute, but only of a unity relative to a plurality of think-able forms" (Ib. 207).

Thus any attempt to raise the "empirical I" to a principle of philosophy is unsuccessful. Our "empirical I," or, shall we say, our every-day self, is only an experiencing being; our "absolute I," or, shall we say, our true self, never comes completely to expression. The reality of our every-day self is determined not through itself but through objects around it. Again, as in our every-day experience we may think of our true self as finding some expression, so Schelling says the "empirical I" is indebted to the causality of the "absolute I" (Ib. 237). As we cannot imagine an act that embodies the whole of our true self without in some way losing ourselves, so Schelling regards the "empirical I" as existing through a limitation of the "absolute I" (Ib. 240). Again, as our true self is not a different kind of self from our every-day self, but our every-day self is but an incomplete or frag-mentary expression of our true self, so Schelling says that the causality of the "empirical I" is distinct from the causality of the "absolute I" quantitatively and not qualitatively; the infinite is of the same kind as the finite (Ib. 240). And finally, as you owe your personality to a unity of consciousness in your every-day experience while your true self remains an indefinable beyond consciousness, so Schelling says, "in the finite I is unity of consciousness, that is, personality" but "the infinite I knows no consciousness, no personality" (Ib. 200).

The "absolute I," than which there is no other God, requires now a positive definition. On the one hand, it is the one original real; on the other hand, it is the infinite ideal. It appears in the first character chiefly in "The I as a Principle of Philosophy," and in the second character chiefly in "Philosophical Letters concerning Dogmatism and Criticism," both of 1795. Not-withstanding Schelling's denunciation of Theology in the name of Philosophy, we cannot overlook the fundamentally religious character of his mystically experienced "real" which is at the same time his eschatologically hoped for "ideal."

To establish the "absolute I" he lays it down as a rule for all knowledge that it must proceed from "immediate experience" (W. I, 1, 318). The mental act by which the "absolute I" is immediately experienced is "intellectual perception" (Ib. 208). This perception of the intellect by the intellect is separated from logical deduction and is presupposed by it. It is not a reflection upon our mental processes but it enters when the "perceiving self is identical with the perceived self," in a moment in which "the pure absolute eternity" is in us (Ib. 319). It is the perception that Spinoza had, but he, in objectifying its object, put the cart before the horse. "Jacobi has described it" (Ib. 318), the spiritual mate of Plato, who could admirably distinguish the absolute, unchangeable Being from every conditioned, changing existence (Ib. 216). Human speech is a poor instrument to tell of this self-grappling contemplativeness. It is set in immediate comparison and contrast with the religious faith of finite natures (Ib.), and the falling away from it is a falling away from original blessedness into sin (Ib. 325-6).

What Schelling has found in this way is not simply the abstraction of an analytic proposition of identity nor that for which the negative term "unconditioned" would be an adequate description, and we may count a score of transcendent epithets with which our young philosopher adorns his "God." Our phrase, the "one, original, real," is an attempt to summarize them.

Firstly, it is absolutely real. He distinguishes carefully between that which exists under general laws and that which exists independent of such limits, namely, pure Being (W. I, 1, 309; 209). In contrast to an objective God who would have to be looked upon as existing in the former sense, the "absolute I" exists in the latter sense. Pure Being is the "highest idea of the ancients," and existence in this sense belongs alone to the "absolute I." Its essential nature is Reality (Ib. 195), and its reality is absolute (Ib. 208). The "secret, marvelous capacity" of our innermost selves convinces us that this Something really *is*, while all else lacks such substantial reality (Ib. 318). It is the only Substance, all else is mere accident (Ib. 192-3).

Secondly, it has absolute unity in itself. It is not one among others, it is neither species nor individual; it has absolute homogeneity (Ib. 184); it does not exist through the actuality of its parts (Ib. 182). It is pure identity (Ib. 177); it is that in which

the principle of being and the principle of thinking coincide
(Ib. 163).

Thirdly, it contains the original causality of all things. Out
of it comes every condition and form of our knowlege (Ib. 162),
it is the fixed point on which hangs everything that is actual
(Ib. 178). "In the I, philosophy, after its struggling, now wins
the highest laurels of its strife; it has found the all-embracing
unity" (Ib. 193); and "the highest idea that the causality of the
absolute I expresses is the idea of absolute might" (Ib. 195).

Although Schelling has claimed that his Idealism is the completion of Kant's Criticism, we are not to suppose that the
problems that Kant found theoretically insoluble are now any
nearer theoretical solution. After Kant had enquired into the
possibility of joining a many into a one in our act of judgment
and found the question theoretically insoluble, it was for the
next thinking man to set the problem in a higher abstraction
(W. I, 1, 175). This problem appears now variously: How comes
the world to exist (Ib. 313)? How pass from the infinite to the
finite (Ib. 314)? Whence comes a sphere of experience (Ib. 310)?
Expressed in its highest abstraction: How does the absolute I go
out of itself and set up a not-I opposed to it (Ib. 175)? This is
the problem which it is the chief business of all philosophy to
solve (Ib. 313). Yet, however variously shaped, and however
pressing, the philosopher can only "untie" this Gordian knot
as Alexander did; its question is "absolutely unanswerable"
(Ib. 311).

The "absolute I," our intellect's most certain and immediate
perception, cannot then, notwithstanding its "absolute might,"
step down from the austere isolation of its unconditioned reality.
Perhaps, however, the going thither is easier than the coming
thence. This is the alternative left to us. If the infinite does
not come down to us we can strive to reach up to the infinite.
The "absolute I" changes from the whence to the whither. "In
the finite is to dwell the tendency, the eternal strife, to lose
itself in the infinite" (W. I, 1, 315). What was the most certain
possession is now to be approached by endless effort; what
actually *is* is ever *becoming*, the "absolute I" is the goal as well
as the starting point of all philosophy (Ib. 240f).

Be absolute,—identical with thyself (Ib. 119)! Strive not to bring yourself nearer to the godhead, but strive infinitely to bring the godhead into yourself (Ib.335). "It is better to struggle and to perish struggling against an absolute might than to ensure oneself against all danger by means of a moral God," this is the "principle of all sublimity" (Ib. 284). Thus he writes to Hegel, of whom he is called "the morning star": "accordingly there is no personal God, and our highest strife is to destroy our personality, to pass over into the sphere of absolute Being— which, however, is not in eternity possible; therefore only a drawing near to the absolute *through action;* and therefore *immortality*" (L. I, 77).

"God, theoretically, is I=not-I, pragmatically, absolute I that negates every not-I. In so far as the infinite I is represented schematically as final goal of the finite I, therefore *outside of* the same, God can be represented in the practical philosophy as *outside of* the finite (schematical) I, but only as identical with the infinite I" (W. I, 1, 201). Thus Schelling's starting point is summarized. Metaphysically, God is an intellectual perception of a unity prior to any separation into the subjective form and the non-subjective content; in finite experience, or practically, God is infinitely approachable. Moreover the only God there is must be expressed in terms of the Self.

But a closer look at the equation will disclose the equal significance of the not-self. He has throughout correlated the "not-I" with the "I," and all that was said for the "not-I" was simply that it was not "I." Yet in the infinite strife of the "I," the "not-I" must be a sphere rich in possibilities for infinite experiencing; and purposeful strife must be able to rely upon nature's organization. Indeed, "so long as finite natures exist, there must also be two systems directly opposed to each other" (W. I, 1, 306). The "two systems" are "Criticism" and "Dogmatism." In the next chapter they become the Transcendental Philosophy and the Philosophy of Nature, the former treating of the "I," the latter of the "not-I."

II

MAN'S ABSOLUTE WILL AND NATURE'S SOUL

(Leipzig, 1796-1798)

After the summer of '95, our philosopher, anxious to realize his hopes for foreign travel, became private tutor to two noble youths whom he was to accompany abroad. Political conditions thwarted his hopes, and in the spring of '96 he accompanied his pupils to Leipzig and there remained. In writing to his parents he reveals his lack of satisfaction with his position, but the church is not considered seriously as an alternative: "for Theology I am not suited, having in the meantime become in no way more orthodox" (L. I, 208). He has written in praise of human dignity and of the sublimity of moral atheism, "the atheism that believes in immortality and denies God" (W. I, 1, 350). He now embraces to the full the opportunity at hand for scientific study and follows enthusiastically courses in mathematics, physics and medicine. In his works of this period (A general Survey of the most recent Philosophical Literature, 1796; Ideas for a Philosophy of Nature, 1797; Upon the World-Soul, 1798) the "absolute I" receives emphasis as "Will" and the "not-I" is fully developed as a cosmos.

A. Schelling's Transcendental Idealism of this period, recognizing that Criticism is not to remain merely Criticism, seeks to "complete" it. If Criticism is taken as a system it can be either Idealism or Realism; but Criticism judged according to its spirit and used as a method leads to the strongest Idealism. To the Idealism thus founded the "practical reason" (i.e. the will) is pre-eminent over the "theoretical reason," and "things-in-themselves" are an inconsistency (W. I, 1, 302-3). We do not present in detail the expansion of his system during this Leipzig period, but we keep in touch with the main stream of thought as it affects our subject.

Schelling's attack upon the "things-in-themselves" of the dogmatizing "Kantians" recalls in its enthusiasm and its motives

the attack by Berkeley upon Locke's "material substances."
"Belief in the original identity of the object and its mental
representation is the *root* of our theoretical and practical understanding. On the other hand, as history might show, the opinion
that there is an original object *outside of* us, of which the idea is
an effect, is the primary source of all scepticism" (W. I, 1, 378).
If behind the reality that *appears*, you look for another reality
belonging primarily to the object, you come across nothing but
negation (Ib. 212).

Instead of such separation between ourselves and the external
world as is involved in a belief in a "thing-in-itself," "we are
compelled to maintain that we do not originally perceive things
outside of us, or, as some have taught, in *God*, but that we perceive them originally in *ourselves*. If this is so, no separation
between the inner and external world is possible" (W. I, 1, 391).
The object is "a real construction of the soul itself" and in this
fact lies finally "all immediacy and thus all certainty of our
knowledge" (Ib. 380). "We do not want nature to meet with the
laws of our minds accidentally (perhaps through the medium of a
third), but we need *nature itself* necessarily and originally, not
only to express, but also to realize the laws of our mind; and it
is only a nature in so far as it does this" (W. I, 2, 56). "The
mind has in itself the absolute means for realizing its existence
and its knowledge, and through what it is in general, it is, in
particular, that to which *nature*, this ordered system of mental
representations of external things, belongs" (W. I, 2, 39).

In close connection with this rejection of the unknowable
thing-in-itself is his opposition to Dogmatism with its faith in an
absolute Object and his equation of the absolute I with the
unconditional freedom of Kant's Critique of Practical Reason.
The thing-in-itself taken as a supersensible ground of phenomena is the leading falsehood of all Dogmatism (W. I, 2, 195),
and it was this which the Theologians deified as an absolute
Object (Ib. 1, 288). Instead of making this "uncomprehended"
into the foremost reality, reality is actually man's unconditioned
Freedom. This is not a "theoretical" solution to the problem of
knowledge but a "practical" one. "Reason has made its
solemn renunciation of discoveries in supernatural regions"

(Ib. 346); freedom, however, leaves no external indeterminable. Man's freedom would be no freedom if the world against which it strives were an Absolute, or if it were not able to determine the world in which it strives.   Freedom is therefore not only itself unconditioned but it is the final existence, which lies at the basis of all that exists, the absolute existence, which reveals itself in every existence (Ib. 179); and of selfconsciousness itself the will is the source (Ib. 401).

It is thus absurd to want to find the fulcrum for the lever of Archimedes "theoretically (that is, in the world itself)"; as Kant says, this firm point is found in the "inner idea of freedom" (W. I, 1, 401). "We postulate the I." "What is it?" "It is not something outside of you to which you can point with your finger. Construct it and you will know what it is, for it is nothing other than what you construct" (Ib. 449-50). Similarly Geometry does not demonstrate space but space is constructed in the construction of figures within it; unlike Geometry, however, Philosophy is without sensuous forms but constructs in pure self-reflecting perception. There is in man pure, unconditioned, absolute, groundless, free activity (Ib. 395). It is the "absolute Will"; this is the "only inconceivable, indissoluble, and according to its nature the most groundless, the most undemonstrable, and just on that account the most immediate and most evident in our knowledge." "In the absolute Will the mind perceives itself immediately, or it has an intellectual perception of itself" (Ib. 400-1).

B. We now pass to Schelling's Philosophy of Nature of this period.   Kuno Fischer indicates its historical significance: "Kant had put into the hand of philosophy the thread of Ariadne by which to penetrate into the labyrinth of nature; Fichte had turned Critical Philosophy into a doctrine of the development of mind; Schelling widens it into a theory of the evolution of nature and the world." Not only in biology is the theory of organic evolution first set up on a philosophical basis and Darwin's theory of adaptation "comprehensively expressed," but also in physics, as Ehrenberg says, "Schelling is Einstein's prophet."

The keynote of this Philosophy of Nature is the conception under which psychology, biology, physics and astronomy can be

coördinated; in the dualism of forces that characterizes all
phenomena. "The first essential of a philosophical theory of
nature is to recognize polarity and dualism in the whole of
nature" (W. I, 2, 459). The two opposing forces are variously
designated. The one is positive (expansive), productive, active,
infinite in itself; the other is negative, attracting, restrictive,
limiting. He corrects the loose way of speaking of matter as
"having" the properties of repulsion and attraction; the forces
themselves are all that matter is (Ib. 23). "In every individual
body the forces of repulsion and attraction are in equilibrium"
(Ib. 186) and of the general system of nature they are the principles (Ib. 187).

Schelling has no thought of remaining satisfied with this
universal dualism, and, as the absolute I or the absolute Will is
the original ground of the opposition between the I and not-I,
so he seeks an original dynamic Substrate behind the opposition
of the forces and from which they go out, an "absolute One"
which is the *prius* of the two. The insoluble problem of his
Transcendental Philosophy was that of the "Absolute going out
of itself"; in his Philosophy of Nature he has been led, this time
inductively, to face the same problem in connection with the
origin of the universal duality. In his Master's thesis, the theme
of which was the Fall of man in the third chapter of Genesis, he
has spoken with respect of that mythology in its attempt to
grapple with the problem of the world's origin, and, in a manu-
script of 1795, has declared that "the only true and thinkable
creation out of nothing" is the "whole world which steps forth
out of nothing with the free selfconscious creature" (*Das älteste
Systemprogramm des deutschen Idealismus. Sitzungsberichte der
Heidelberger Akadamie der Wissenschaften*, p. 14, 5 Abh. 1917).

Can nature now be regarded as the production of one force
instead of two? He selects one of the two forces. They have
never been regarded as of equal rank. The former, as given
above, is named "the first," the latter becomes "the second."
Also, in the conceptions "positive" and "negative," an inherent
superiority belongs to the former. While the "positive" determines that there shall be conditions of existence, the "negative"
only prescribes conditions without which there could be no exist-

ence. The "positive" is "living," the "negative" is "dead." The "positive" becomes that by which alone all the facts can be explained, and in contrast to this, which is an infinite in itself but determinable, the "negative" is that which determines by providing limits. We can further make the "positive" into a unity and speak of it as the one supreme condition, while the negative becomes plural, and is thus a mass of conditions (Cf. W. I, 2, 408). Again, the "positive" is linked with the organic and the "negative" with the mechanical, and nature is conceived as primarily an organism; "not, where no mechanism is, is organism, but, on the contrary, where no organism is, is mechanism" (W. I, 1, 349).

After that attempt to follow Schelling in getting beyond the universal dualism to the universal unity which is not at all thought of as the relativity of the two, we present some account of this One. "The positive in itself is the absolute One; it is the age-long idea of a primal matter (the ether), which broadens itself out in countless phenomena like the many single beams broken in an infinite prism" (W. I, 2, 395). The more poetical term for this "absolute One" is "World-Soul." This term comes from the Greeks, whose mythology was a historical schematization of nature (Ib. 1, 472). This "soul" of things is not "mind" but a physical "force," and its synonyms are "ether," "light-ether," "matter," or "absolute matter." Again, it is not the world-process itself, for this consists in the operation of a duality of opposing forces; it is the "organizing principle shaping the world into a system" (Ib. 2, 381). Finally, brought before this "absolute One," "we stand still in quietness before that Unknown in which the oldest philosophy has erstwhile felt the Primal Force of nature" (Ib. 568).

The foregoing image of nature has come out of his Transcendental Philosophy. "Since in our mind there is an infinite strife to organize itself, so must there be in the external world a universal tendency towards organization" (W. I, 1, 386). Our whole knowledge, and with it the whole of nature in the manifold variety of its aspects arises out of infinite approximations to that x (the real), and the world finds its endurance only in our eternal strife to give it definition (Ib. 2, 219). Mind, as "invisible nature," has as its counterpart, nature as "visible mind."

It would be fascinating enough to follow the operation of the two forces forming every product of nature, seeing them in mechanical equilibrium in the primal light, finding them disturbed, yet continually restored in every chemical action and reaction in "infinite production and reproductions," and again observing their struggle in the last life of nature's "noblest form" where their successive organic equilibrium and differentiation constitute man's life-process—a process ceasing when they are finally hindered in their restoration. Such natural strife, process, evolution, is like the endless struggle of the human mind to approach infinitely the absolute reality. Not only, however, in the infinite strife of opposing forces have we found nature an analogue of mind. This period has offered us two absolute forces, the one "inconceivable" and the other "unknown," "quite beyond the limits of all possible perception" (Ib. 381), an Absolute of Mansoul and an Absolute of Worldsoul. Such "stillness" as we are asked to observe before the Absolute of Worldsoul is disturbed by the reflection that, while the Absolute of Mansoul is its archetype, yet Mansoul itself appears as a late product of nature, as that in which the "successive stages of nature's life" reach their highest!

III

Unconscious Productivity

(*Jena, 1798-1800*)

In July '98 Schelling received from Goethe the announcement
of his appointment as Lecturer at the University of Jena. Fichte,
who had been there for four years, and who was to remain there
a fifth, during which he was to face a charge of Atheism, influ-
enced Schelling's appointment, as also did Niethammer. During
August Schelling spent six weeks in Dresden where birds of a
feather were met together to admire its art treasures. Here he
first met Caroline, who was to be his Muse for a decade. Her
husband, A. W. Schlegel, who had been engaged for two years
upon his celebrated translation of Shakespeare, was there, as
also his brother Friedrich, and Hardenberg and Gries. Schelling
was welcomed as having much in common with the nascent
Romantic School of German poetry.

He commenced his work at Jena in October. In the following
year he was invited by Goethe to spend with him the last Christ-
mas of the eighteenth century. He stayed over for the New
Year festivals, and the fifty-year-old Goethe, the forty-year-old
Schiller, and the twenty-five-year-old Schelling saw together the
dawn of the nineteenth century (L. I, 297). Of Schelling's
lectures upon the Philosophy of Art Windelband remarks that
by their influence upon the Jena circle they determined the whole
future development of Aesthetics.

A poem of Schelling's exhibits his strong antipathy against the
mystico-religious turn that Romanticism took in Schleiermacher
and Novalis. As Wordsworth later found the "anchor" of his
purest thoughts and soul of all his moral being in "nature and
the things of sense," so a few lines from Schelling will illustrate
his "enthusiasm for irreligion" as the younger Schlegel dubbed
it:

"No church will I visit to hear them preach,
I have done with all the parsons teach.
Yet there's a faith that masters my will,
Glows in my verse, and inspires me still.

Here on the earth, in her blue eyes see
The deepest depths that exist for me.

I am the God who nature's bosom fills,
I am the life that in her heart blood thrills.

Onwards, to where, in thought's eternal truth
Nature's deep self re-words itself in truth,
There stirs one might, one pulse-beat all sufficing,
All power retaining, aye,—and sacrificing."

                    (L. I, 285-7. Royce's translation.)

To fulfill the demands of careful exegesis, we have already, in the heading of this chapter, represented the Schelling of 1800 as having already passed beyond the position in which the Philosophy of Nature can be subsumed under the Transcendental Philosophy. He has not, however, recognized this (W. I, 3, 11; 14). We are thus faced with a working over of the two Philosophies, with re-annunciations and re-colorings of the Absolute, and his writings use a terminology which, while it is drawn from the position which he is consciously holding, expresses ideas that are only consistent with the position to which he is advancing.

"The Philosophy of Nature treats of Nature as Transcendental Philosophy treats of the I." From both of these Philosophies an unconditioned, original, objective Being is excluded (Ib. 12), and in both we find the one Absolute, for which we suggest "unconscious Productivity" as the designation most true to his real position at this stage of his work. The Philosophy of Nature is now presented first.

A. Nature is organic (W. I, 3, 33-4) as well as dynamical and the highest principle for its explanation is "Productivity." This is clothed with the special kind of being that is peculiar to an absolute. It has no formal existence. It is not Nature as "object" but Nature as "subject." Productivity is absolutely non-objective (Ib. 284). Nature as "subject" is "pure Being or Productivity itself" (Ib. 285). The product (the object) is evanescent but the productivity (the subject) remains (Ib. 13-14), and is the original absolute infiniteness (Ib. 14-16). In this aspect nature has "unconditioned reality"; its laws are not prescribed to it by any other Being, it is the Law-giver to itself and sufficient in itself (Ib. 17). Again, this Productivity is absolute unity (Ib. 63); and it is the efficient and final cause of nature (Ib. 27).

This "absolute Productivity" is recognized by a method more sober than that by which he set up his first Absolute. "We know nothing except through experience" (W. I, 3, 278). Though the Absolute cannot be "known" it can be "recognized" as that which *is;* "we do not *know* nature, but nature *is a priori*" (Ib. 279). This *a priori natura naturans* is not merely a probability or an hypothesis, but something that is most evident and certain (Ib.). How else could Speculative Physics be true to its name as the "mother of all great discoveries" (Ib. 280), and in experimenting (in the phrase now famous) "put a question to nature" (Ib. 276), if things were not known through the "principles of their possibility" (Ib. 275)?

As only a "unity," however, this cosmogonic Productivity can produce no product. In fact "the conception of the product (the fixed) and the conception of the productivity (the free) are mutually opposed" (Ib. 299). Before dealing with this crucial problem we stop to observe that here the "absolute ether" appears again, and now as the first original product (Ib. 33); it is the ground-type lying at the basis of all products (Ib. 300). This "absolute fluid" matter evolves itself in an infinite series of developing forms, in an infinite metamorphosis (Ib. 297; 300). Thus Hoelderin celebrates it: "O father Ether! True and friendly; no God nor Mother has nurtured me as Thou" (Koeber).

The "main problem of the Philosophy of Nature is not to explain activity in nature (for that is very easily conceived because it is nature's first pre-supposition), but to explain the resting, the permanent" (W. I, 3, 18). However hard Schelling felt the pressure of this "main problem" we hope his auditors found it more consistently dealt with than the larger public for

whom he did not originally write (Ib. 4). He stands by the principle of modern logic, "all determination is negation" (Ib. 287).
Any thought of a product is the thought of confining within
limits the absolute Productivity. Whence this limiting? It
cannot come from *outside* of nature, for nature is the only original,
absolute Productivity; and how can it arise *within* nature, when
nature is so defined?

Twice he offers the illustration of a vortex (Ib. 18; 289).
Imagine a river. It flows onward in "pure identity" until it
meets with an opposition; then a whirlpool forms. "Every
original product of nature is such a whirlpool," it is in every
instant disappearing, and in every instant it is there. Nature
is an infinite number of such points of limitation in which productivity is negated. This is an illustration of his "atomism."
These atoms are not those of the mechanical physicist whose
"mechanical simples" are unthinkable (Ib. 244), they are dynamical atoms, they are "monads"; "every original action represents,
as it were, a natural monad" (Ib. 22-3), and "in each lies the
germ of a universe"(Ib. 291). This monadistic solution, however, though not condemned, appears to be discredited (Vide ib.
244; 296).

He now glides into a solution that demands a duplexity in the
original unity. Although the Productivity is negated, that
which negates must, in its way, be positive, "that which limits is
an activity" (W. I, 3, 42). Affirming the "original identity" of
nature, the "highest problem of natural science" is "to explain
what original cause in the universal identity of nature has
brought that infinite opposition and thereby the conditioning
of the universal motion" (Ib. 161). The organism proves to be a
"duplexity" (Ib. 148); polarity is "identity in duplexity and
duplexity in identity" (Ib. 218). "There is postulated, therefore, a common cause of the general and organic duplexity"
(Ib. 220), an "absolute duplexity" (Ib. 219). This "ultimate
cause of the natural phenomenon is not itself a phenomenon";
nor is it a "mere hypothesis." "The totality of nature is not
simply an aggregation but a necessary nature" and "that
oscillation of nature between productivity and product must
appear as a universal duplexity of principles"; "universal

duality, as a principle for explaining nature, is as necessary as the concept of nature itself" (Ib. 277).

Even this does not satisfy us. The absolute Productivity $(P=P)$ divides itself into two activities, the positive (P) and the negative (N). The product is to represent these activities in a composite unity or "equilibrium" $(P=N)$. Since, however, the absolute Productivity is not to come to cessation in any product, he also makes the composite unity or state of "equilibrium" (Ib. 310) a differentiated unity, or state of "indifference" $(P \neq N)$!

Again, the construction of the product is turned into the mathematical conception of a limit. "Nature as object is that which comes out of an infinite series" (W. I, 3, 288). This conception, however, is to apply not to any individual product but to nature as a whole. "All individual organizations together are to be accepted as only one product" (Ib. 63); "there is only one product which lives in all products" (Ib. 54). This product is infinite; "absolute activity can be represented not by means of a finite product, but only by means of an infinite product" (Ib. 14). *Natura naturata* is a final goal, which "*becomes* and never is" (Ib. 16; 20), an ever becoming product (Ib. 33). The productivity of nature is "absolute continuity" and the product passes through "infinite metamorphoses" (Ib. 300) in pursuit of a "common ideal" to which it infinitely approximates (Ib. 69; 33; 64), of an absolute organization for which it longs and continually strives to represent (Ib. 43).

Thus from the "absolute Productivity" (Nature as "subject") which stood at the beginning, our view is directed to the "absolute Product" (Nature as "object") which stands at the infinite end. The "empirical infiniteness is infinite becoming" (W. I, 3, 285), and though it "never exists" it can be recognized as the only possible explanation of the approximations to it as exemplified in comparative anatomy and physiology (Ib. 64f). The story of the infinite process is told by Natural History, which "has for its object not the *products* but *nature itself*, and pursues the *one* Productivity" (Ib. 291). "What is the earth? Its history is interwoven into the history of nature as a whole, and thus goes upwards from the fossil through the inorganic and

organic nature to the history of the universe—one chain"
(Ib. 307). The last chapter of this history will never be written.
Physics will never completely fulfill its one task of filling up the
gaps in the continuous whole, for every new discovery will throw
us back into a new unknown, each elucidation carry with it
another complication, and thus "our science itself is an infinite
task."

B. Schelling now presents his Transcendental Philosophy of
1800 in the "System of Transcendental Idealism," and, as five
years earlier, we have again an infinite Unconditioned as the
final ground of knowledge. This "principle of all Reality"
(W. I, 3, 375) is the "I yonside of consciousness" (Ib. 380),
an "original activity going forth into infinity" (Ib. 385). As
"Being itself" no predicates belong to it (Ib. 600), and thus "is
the paradox explained that we cannot say that it is," but we can
say that it gives existence to all things. It requires no other
being to carry it for it bears and supports itself (Ib. 376). It
brings all actions to an harmonious goal (Ib. 598) and is itself
raised above the antithesis of necessity and freedom and is the
common source of both. It is the ground of the identity of subject and object; it is the invisible root of which all intelligences
are only the potencies (Ib. 600), the highest absolutely Real
which never becomes objective but is the cause of everything
that does (Ib. 615).

We have reached the point where the I-designation of the Absolute has become inappropriate, though it remains the one most
frequently given. Schelling is on his way to that "dawn" in
whose light he openly breaks with Fichte's "subjective Idealism."
The reader can already see the rays of the approaching day more
brightly than the writer who works in the morning twilight. The
objective idealism of the foregoing philosophy of nature cannot
now be gainsaid. Behind the opening paragraphs of the "Transcendental Idealism" is the assumption that the Transcendental
Philosophy can be treated as a Philosophy of Nature (W. I, 3,
399f), and other references show that he is not Fichte's disciple.
Nature is an intelligence which has not come to maturity (Ib. 341).
A "true and complete philosophy" can only copy in freedom the
original that necessity has wrought (Ib. 397). Above all, the

puzzling sentence, "Yonside of consciousness is the I *mere* objectivity" (Ib. 380) can only be made intelligible by making it say that the "absolute I" has become "Nature."

For the formula for his "idealism" Schelling suggests the un-grammatical "I is" to avoid the inadequate "I am" (L. I, 170), but the function ascribed to it now shows the inappropriateness of the I-designation. It is the Absolute that is the "something common to the actions of all men" (W. I, 3, 598). We therefore see in the Transcendental Philosophy the same absolute as appears in the Philosophy of Nature. "The I appears, sub-jectively, as infinite productivity; objectively, as eternal be-coming." This "I," as was "Productivity" is "Being itself" (Ib. 376), and again, as was the Productivity, the I "yonside of consciousness" is "originally non-objective;" it is "pure pro-ducing going into infinity" (Ib. 380).

To represent this deity, this "eternal Unconscious, which, like an eternal sun in the constellation of minds, is hidden by the brilliance of its light" (W. I, 3, 600), as a mere abstraction is the "crudest misunderstanding of idealism, and is no better than representing it as a substantial or personal Being" (Ib. 333).

In the "System of Transcendental Idealism" the division of the whole of Philosophy into the Theoretical, the Practical, and the Philosophy of Art reminds us of the three Critiques of Kant. The work may be regarded as offering respectively a philosophy of the Unconscious, of the Conscious, and of the Unconscious-Con-scious. There are three stages of productivity; or, using more familiar terms, we have (A) the passivity of the mind in which it owes its knowledge to the activity of nature or of things as they are, (B) an activity of the mind in which it constructs nature, or affects things according to its will, and (C) a situation where passivity and activity stand in mutual relation, where nature and mind embrace each other. This threefold division we follow in completing this chapter.

(A) In our two previous chapters, as also already in this, we have observed the sweep of Schelling's thought from the ready-made Absolute that stands at the beginning to the Abso-lute in the making that stands at the "end" of an infinite prog-ress. "A system is complete when it comes back to its starting point" (W. I, 3, 628). We have also felt his greater concern for the initial Absolute, and as such it now finds systematic placing in the "theoretical philosophy." Before the philosopher has reached that stage of reflection when, in an act of selfconsciousness, he says "I am," he is a sharer in life's way, a part of nature's unconscious activity. When the stage of selfconsciousness is attained, he now repeats the unconscious in consciousness, he thinks God's thoughts after him. "The philosophical gift exists chiefly in the ability to reproduce freely in consciousness the original necessary (unconscious) activity" (Ib. 397-8). Thus is explained how beautifully the external world is fitted to the mind. "Because our knowledge is wholly and thoroughly empirical it is on that account wholly and completely *a priori*," and "because it is wholly and completely *a priori*, it is wholly and completely empirical" (Ib. 528). "The progress from thesis to antithesis and on to synthesis (selfconsciousness) is grounded originally in the mechanism of the mind" (Ib. 394), acting "completely unconsciously" (Ib. 529).

When philosophy contemplates this harmony between the objective world that is fitted to our mental representations and the mental representations that are fitted to the objective world, it must postulate a ground for this harmony. The act of selfconsciousness itself, without which there is no philosophy, must be a reproduction of what has existed in the natural, unconscious mind. Since in the act of selfconsciousness there is brought together the subject and the object in a single judgment in which the subject is also the object, there must be an original, unconscious identity of subject and object. "If we could think, for example, of an action in God, it must be absolutely free, and this absolute freedom would be at the same time absolute necessity. Such an act is the original act of selfconsciousness" (W. I, 3, 395). We cannot know this Absolute; we know about it through inference (Ib. 396-7). It is the *a priori* by which alone selfconsciousness, and thus philosophy itself, is possible.

Schelling's monistic foundation remains ever imperturbable. Yet, as in the Philosophy of Nature, in order to account for a product, an "absolute duality" followed close upon the heels of the "absolute unity" of Productivity, so here, the "I yonside of consciousness," the "absolute identity in which there is no duplexity" (Ib.600), in which, like the self of Hindu philosophy, "nothing is distinguished" (Ib. 402), must differentiate itself into two "activities" in order to explain the "product" of the Transcendental Philosophy, the philosopher's act of selfconsciousness. "Selfconsciousness is a synthetic act," it is "subject and object together" (Ib. 391). Since the "I of selfconsciousness" is thus a "struggle of opposite tendencies" (Ib. 392) we are confronted by a necessary dualism. "As a physicist, Descartes said, Give me matter and motion and I shall therewith furnish for you the universe. The transcendental philosopher says, Give me a nature of opposing activities, the one going into infinity and the other striving to intuit itself in this infinity, and I shall let arise for you thereout the intelligence with its whole system of ideas" (Ib. 427). "The condition of all consciousness is duplexity" (Ib. 600). His theory of magnetism, which placed the seat of the positive and negative forces in the positive (the north) pole (Ib. 446) affords a happy illustration. The two activities "must be an absolute One" (Ib. 386).

Is selfconsciousness thereby accounted for? Kant had provided the problem. On the one hand, "I am" is a judgment which excludes any object except the "I" making the judgment; on the other hand, the "I am" implies also "I am not . . .," the analytical unity of selfconsciousness is possible only in relation to the synthetic unity of the consciousness of objects. Or, on the one hand, selfconsciousness involves a removal of all relation to that which has difference in itself; on the other hand, selfconsciousness is only possible through the existence of such relations. "In the I," says Schelling, "are original opposites, subject and object; they cancel each other, and yet one is not possible without the other" (Ib. 393). Hence arises the struggle "between the incapacity of uniting infinite opposites on the one hand, and, on the other hand, the necessity of doing so if the identity of consciousness is not to be canceled" (Ib. 394).

The kind of selfconsciousness that Schelling has in mind is an "absolute synthesis," an act in which "all conditions of consciousness arise at the same time" (Ib. 410). It would have been true enough to the parallel with the Philosophy of Nature

if the achievement of such a selfconsciousness had been represented as an infinite task. In fact, we read of the "organizing
intelligence which ever seeks the absolute point of equilibrium,
which point, however, lies in infinity" (Ib. 480-1), and of a
totality of actions as the condition of selfconsciousness (Ib. 560).
This, however, would have left us with a selfconsciousness that
is at once necessary to begin with and in no finite time attainable.

No, the "equilibrium" must be attained at a definite point
in time. But what we were dissatisfied with previously is again
with us. Selfconsciousness, which "is to be thought of not
as the negation of the two activities but as their equilibrium"
or composite unity $(S=O)$, is also a *"third* activity" (Ib. 399 ff.)
or differentiated unity $(S \neq O$, cf. above p. 24)!

It turns out that the problem is not to be solved wholly by
the "theoretical philosophy" and its solution takes us into the
"practical philosophy." Selfconsciousness, we repeat, is an act
"in which all conditions of consciousness arise at the same time."
These "conditions" are analyzable into two aspects, "a limitedness in general," which gives an identity of subject and object,
from which identity all other subjects and objects are excluded,
and "a particular limitedness" by which *this* individual is distinguished, not from "selfless objects," but from other individuals. In the first aspect, the subject and object are viewed
together; in the second aspect, the subject-object becomes an
object. The first aspect is theoretically explicable. The "beginning of consciousness" is "an absolute abstraction" (Ib. 533).
The absolute will has worked as a driving force in my mind's
natural mechanism producing my unconscious activity. As
existing in me unconsciously, "the original act of selfconsciousness
falls outside of time" (Ib. 537). It is this "original autonomy"
which is the "first principle of all philosophy" (Ib. 535).

According to the second aspect, i. e., the recognition of the
self as object among other objects, a "particular limitedness" is
demanded of the same act of selfconsciousness, and it falls
"within a definite point of time" (Ib. 538). "That the particular
limitedness cannot be determined through the limitedness in
general and yet that the particular limitedness arises at the same
time and through the same act as the limitedness in general, is the

inconceivable and inexplicable of philosophy" (Ib. 410). Unlike the first aspect, this second aspect is "undeniably inexplicable by anything that has transpired in the (unconscious) intelligence" (Ib. 538).

(B) We are now in the "practical philosophy." The limitation required must come from outside. The recognition of one's own individuality is only possible in reference to other individuals, "through the same act by means of which I observe myself to be limited in my free action, other intelligences already exist" (Ib. 546). This pragmatic solution demands that the other intelligences set the limits to the individual will. This means that selfconsciousness is a "social contrast effect" (Royce: *Lectures on Modern Idealism*, p. 128). That is true of selfconsciousness in its relative aspect. It means also, if we are not to ignore its "absolute" aspect, what is of more significance to us. We recall the "monadistic" phase where there was an infinite number of "points of restriction." If now the monism is to stand, we cannot postulate as many "cores of the universe" or absolute autonomies as there are human beings in history. The "negative" activity was itself one side of the "absolute Productivity." This solution must mean, therefore, that the "absolute I" exists apart from the selfconsciousness of any individual and works as an unconscious Productivity common to all.

Since the whole is an "absolute Product," we turn again from the problem of the beginning to that of the end, and there "shines" the "Absolute" as the "completion" of an infinite task. The goal of History is an "Areopagus of peoples, composed of all civilized nations" (W. I, 3, 587). How is it to be guaranteed? "The highest, but not unsolved task of Transcendental Philosophy" is for "freedom to become necessity and necessity to become freedom" (Ib. 594). A "moral world-order" is not an adequate solution. "I demand something absolutely objective which, entirely independent of freedom, secures, and, as it were, guarantees the highest goal"; "thus I see myself driven to an Unconscious" by which the completed purpose of history is guaranteed (Ib. 597). Though men are "composers and not mere actors" in the drama, yet "a hidden necessity" must be presupposed operating within human freedom (Ib. 595), which will "produce at the end something rational and harmonious" (Ib.598).

Whatever terms Schelling may now use with regard to what would be if the end were reached, they can only mean, interpreted in the light of his whole present position, that nature's unconscious Productivity becomes all in all. This, however, does not mean that the "subjective" (human freedom) is annihilated, "which is the system of *Fatalism*"; nor does it mean that the "objective" (hidden necessity) is denied, "which is the system of irreligion or of *Atheism*" (Ib. 601). Both freedom and necessity remain. The "eternal Unconscious" is the ground of their pre-established harmony (Ib. 600).

We thus learn what religion is, "in the true meaning of the word." Its God "never *is*"; "if he *were*, then we were not. But he *reveals* himself progressively." There is no completed proof for the existence of God; there is only the "progressive proof," "which can be completed through the whole of history" (Ib. 603). He can never be an object of knowledge, but only an "object of the eternal presupposition in action, that is of faith." The true religion is a "system of Providence" (Ib. 601).

(C) The philosophy of the conscious-unconscious remains. The "harmony" of the two "activities" finds expression in a work of Art. As any natural organism expresses the unity of teleology and mechanism without consciousness, the product of art expresses the unity consciously. "The work of Art reflects to us the identity of the conscious and the unconscious." "Its fundamental character is an unconscious infinite, a synthesis of nature and freedom" (W. I, 3, 619). What "Providence" is in Religion, "Genius" is in Art. "Genius is for Aesthetics what the I is for Philosophy, namely, the highest absolute Real, which never becomes objective, but is the cause of everything objective" (Ib. 619). Within the artist is felt an "infinite opposition," the "*pati Deum*," the inability to bring together the two activities, the unconscious-determined and the conscious-free. This opposition drives him to expression. Then follows an "infinite satisfaction" in the artist, and his product is an "infinite harmony" (Ib. 617). At this standpoint, "God" must be Beauty, and the Superman the Artist.

The motive that seeks to show us the infinite in finite form is both profound and illuminating. Beneath the enthusiasm with which Schelling seizes upon Art—"Art is the only true and eternal organon of philosophy, and at the same time its document" (Ib. 627); "Art opens for the philosopher the Holy of Holies" (Ib. 628)—and writes the inspired hymn which closes the treatise, beneath this "aesthetic idealism" as Windelband terms it, but which could be as well termed "aesthetic realism," there lies, we feel, an attempt to meet the perplexities the system as a whole presents. The "absolute Productivity" that is placed cosmogonically at the beginning of creation and eschatologically at the end of history now finds expression in concrete form; the "absolutely non-objective" can be known in an object, the *absolute* product is known through *this* product. Between the two infinites there is an expression of the Absolute in time, not only in "selfconsciousness" which is intuited by the intellect only, but also in the "product of Art," in "Greek Mythology" for instance (Ib. 619), which any pair of eyes can read.

IV

THE WORLD-SELF'S UNITY

(*Jena, 1800-1803*)

During the second half of Schelling's stay in Jena, which commenced in October, 1800, his lectures grew in popularity until, in his last semester there, the winter of 1802-3, he had two hundred students in attendance (L. I, 432). Jointly with Hegel, who, "older in years, younger in works," comes to Jena in 1801 and contributes to the Schelling-Fichtean controversy an essay "Concerning the Difference between Fichte's and Schelling's System of Philosophy," he published the short-lived "Critical Journal of Philosophy." At the founding of the University of Landshut in 1802, the Medical Faculty nominated Schelling for an honorary doctor's degree as the man who had rendered greatest service to the study of medical science. He has now become "the lion of German philosophy."

During these years he is living and working under the illumination of a "light that first shone upon him in 1801" (L. II, 60; cf. W. I, 7, 144). We have already anticipated this insight. The Transcendental Philosophy and the Philosophy of Nature are to be coördinated in the philosophy of an "Absolute" which is neither "I" nor "Nature" but an original unity that expresses itself in both. This is an "Idealism," by which is not meant that my perception produces a tree that was planted fifty years ago (W. I, 4, 83) but that "all philosophizing consists in the recollecting of the condition in which we were one with nature," that all conscious knowledge is a "reproduction" of nature and is nature's highest expression (Ib. 77). In contrast with Fichte's "Subjective Idealism" it could be termed "Objective Idealism" (Ib. 109).

This change was implied earlier when "nature's first force" was likened to "man's absolute will" and later when social history required a transcendental interchange of human wills. Now that Schelling recognizes that the Philosophy of Nature is no longer subordinate to the Transcendental Philosophy their relation is changed. "The true direction" becomes "that which nature itself has taken" (Ib. 78). This priority ascribed to the Philosophy of Nature must be understood only genetically; a new central aim is to determine his interest in the various sciences, namely, "the free and undisturbed investigation into the depth of the Absolute" (Ib. 401, cf. 5, 282). "I have always previously represented the Philosophy of Nature and the Transcendental Philosophy as opposite poles of philosophy," "now I find myself at the point of neutrality between them" (Ib. 4, 108). The best designation, therefore, of his new position is "subjective-objective" or "absolute Idealism." The Absolute is now the common starting point of the two philosophies and "philosophy is the systematized knowledge of the Absolute" (Ib. 2, 66; A. D. 1802).

By his System of Identity, as Schelling's new position is commonly termed in the history of philosophy, "he solved more perfectly than any before him the first problem of modern philosophy, that of Real-Idealism and Ideal-Realism" (J. E. Erdmann). "The first step towards philosophy is the insight that the absolute-ideal is also the absolute-real" (W. I, 2, 58). In the "Absolute" these opposites are united, it is the "One" of all philosophy (Ib. 4, 321). At earlier standpoints three leading designations of the pure original unity, as we have called it, have offered themselves: (1) the absolute I, (2) absolute Will, (3) unconscious Productivity or Nature as "subject." We have also found that each of these initial unities had a composite unity set in contrast to it: (1) I and not-I, (2) positive and negative activities, (3) duplexity in nature as product or "object." Again, we have found that these composite unities (S = O) had to change into differentiated unities (S ≠ O) to give reality to particular existences and to human endeavor.

He now affirms an "Absolute" which is not only, as are the others, a pure unity (S = S), but which is also at the same time a perfectly balanced or composite unity (S = O), and carries within itself the capacity for becoming and developing (S ≠ O). To the "absolute knowledge" the two opposites (S & O) are not irreconcilable antitheses (Ib. 381); they do not exist in the nature of things but are simply a duality set up by reflection and required by consciousness for its thought-processes (Ib. 257; 381). These opposites appear in different contexts as "infinite and finite," "universal and particular," "mind and nature," "thought and extension," "thinking and being," "conception and perception," "truth and beauty," "divine and natural," "subject and object," or, in the terms above quoted, as "the absolute-ideal and the absolute-real."

At the new standpoint the previous absolutes run together. The "absolute I" of our first chapter now loses its subjective flavor and becomes the World-Self, or the "Universe," or "pure Subject-Object" (Ib. 5, 147; 4, 377). In our last chapter the "unconscious Productivity," the initial *natura naturans* or nature as "subject," was distinguished from the ever-becoming *natura naturata* or nature as "object;" but now that *natura naturans* contains the composite unity (of which *natura naturata* is now the differentiated unity), it too is now designated "pure Subject-Object" (Ib. 4, 86). Thus the Absolute of our first chapter and the Absolute of our last chapter are identical and are used as synonyms (Ib. 4, 327).

This World-Self or "pure Subject-Object" (S = O) is the "universe" not as to its "essence" but as to its "form." The inner or "divine" *essence* of the universe "can only be thought of as absolute, pure and untroubled identity" (W. I, 4, 374). If we have spoken of the "unity of the ideal and real," the antithetical terms are but anticipations of an opposition as yet undistinguished in the original pure unity (S = S). Schelling's first thought is "not of that in which all opposites have been united and abolished, but of that in which all opposites are one, or, rather, have never been separated" (Ib. 235), of "the absolutely simple, pure, and without division" (Ib. 378). This inner essence of the World-Self is an "abyss of rest and inactivity" (Ib. 34); to define it in terms of activity is "to be farthest from the idea of it" (Ib. 303). It is that "highest unity which we consider as a holy abyss" (Ib. 258), or as a "subterranean God" that dwells in its depths (Ib. 329).

"The universe is the absolute identity according to the essence *and* the form of its being" (W. I, 4, 130). "The essence of the

Absolute is also its form and its form its essence" (Ib. 2, 63).
"The absolute or eternal form is, as the absolute itself, absolute
identity, absolutely simple" (Ib. 4, 378). "God and the universe
are one, or only different aspects of one and the same." "God is
the universe considered from the side of identity," "the universe
is God considered from the side of totality" (Ib. 5, 366). "The
absolute identity is not the cause of the universe but the universe
itself" (Ib. 4, 129). The burden of these phrases—their elucidation
will follow—is the insistence that the non-spacial, non-temporal
Universe (or God) must be considered, in regard to its "essence"
as a pure unity (S = S), and in regard to its "form" as a composite unity (S = O); and though our attention may be turned
now to its ideal side, now to its real side, the universe is not
essentially two, but one; and this All-One, being the All as well
as the One, stands in no causal relation with anything outside of
it; "nothing is outside of it" (Ib. 4, 133).

It is possible to mistake this present development for a falling
back into the Spinozistic "Dogmatism" of an "absolute Object"
(Cf. O. Pfleiderer: *Development of Theology since Kant*, p. 63).
As indicated by the terms already used, nature is neither merely
"objective" nor "subjective" but is both in one; the "subjective" and the "objective" are the two sides of its "form."
According to the previous position the "unconscious Productivity" produced, at its highest stage or "potency," consciousness in man. Since, then, "nature has from afar had the natural
tendency to attain the height it reaches through reason" (W. I,
4, 76), the "history of selfconsciousness" can be traced back into
the "unconscious." "Idealism will remain, but it will derive
its beginnings out of nature itself" (Ib. 88). Since the course of
nature produces the "subject-object" relationship in consciousness nature itself must be considered as a knowledge-
process. (Watson criticizes Schelling for coördinating "nature"
and "intelligence" instead of subordinating the former to the
latter. Op. cit. p. 200; 216. But if "nature" *is* "intelligence"
they are not coördinated but are identical; Schelling would not
coördinate nature as unconscious intelligence with nature as
conscious intelligence in man). Nature is an "I" reduced to a
lower power, or "depotentiated" (Ib. 85); a "subject-object"

which, since it is without consciousness (Cf. ib. 4, 256), is "*pure
subject-object*" (Ib. 2, 86).

Schelling continues to demand "intellectual perception" on
the part of the philosopher. "Without intellectual perception
no philosophy!" (Ib. 5, 255). "No one has traced with such
clarity and definiteness the condition under which alone apodic-
tically certain knowledge is possible" (von Hartmann). This
act of observing immediately the operation of reason is now
traced to its roots in *nature's* act, with which the philosopher's
"intellectual perception is one, and of which the mathemati-
cian's science is a copy" (Ib.). "I demand of the Philosophy of
Nature," as it was demanded of the Transcendental Philosophy,
"intellectual perception" (Ib. 4, 87). It is thus that nature,
the "depotentiated I," has "absolute egoity" (Ib. 325). It is
the purely unconscious act from which the human perceiver is
abstracted (Ib. 88). Through what may seem the impenetrable
obscurity of Schelling's demand the motive at least shines clearly
enough. Nature considered as "pure subject-object" delivers us
from the subjectivism that makes nature the product of its late
arrival, human consciousness, and from the "Dogmatism" that
makes nature a thing-in-itself and thus denies to nature the possibility of effecting human consciousness. "The Absolute is the
supreme presupposition of knowledge and is itself the original
knowledge" (Ib. 5, 216).

This application of the principles of knowledge to nature
itself culminates in an account of the universe, as to its "form"
or as a composite unity, in terms of so much "subjectivity" or
"ideality' and so much "objectivity" or "reality." The Universe is the "absolute totality" of the two sides. In distinction
from nature as expressed in its process of development, nature
as a universe or completed whole exhibits a perfect or composite
unity of its two sides $(S = O)$. This composite unity, this
"eternal nature, is the essence of God introduced into the form"
(W. I, 2, 66). Thus the pure original unity $(S = S)$ is equated
with the composite unity; "essence is form and form is essence."
In other words, in distinction from the "relative totality"
$(S \neq O)$ in which the distinction of the "form" from the "essence" will become significant, in the "absolute totality"

(S = O), "form" is indistinguishable from "essence." In Schelling's words, introducing our parentheses: "Could we see in their totality all existing things, we should see in the whole a perfect quantitative equilibrium of subjectivity and objectivity (S = O), therefore nothing except pure identity in which nothing is distinguishable (S = S)" (Ib. 4, 127). As a knowledge-process of a World-Self, the "form" of the universe is the perfect equilibrium or composite unity of "subject" and "object" (S = O); and since "form" can be equated with "essence," this "absolute Knowing" is also the pure original unity (S = S): "the absolute knowledge is the absolute essence" (Ib. 303); there is not an absolute knowledge and outside of this still an Absolute, but both are one (Ib. 404).

This "absolute Knowing" is "absolute Reason." "Absolute Reason" is reason from which the conscious human reasoner has been abstracted, and "reason in so far as it is considered as total indifference of the subjective and the objective" (W. I, 4, 114; "indifference" here is the composite unity, S = O; contrast p. 25 above). Reason may thus be equated with the absolute knowledge, and thus with both the "form" and the "essence" of the universe; in short, "Reason is the Absolute," "outside of Reason is nothing and in it is everything" (Ib. 115); it is the "only in-itself" (Ib. 125). Hence "the standpoint of philosophy is the standpoint of Reason; its knowledge is of things as they are in themselves, i. e. as they are in Reason" (Ib. 115). (This exposition differs from von Hartmann, who says Schelling equates Reason with the idea of the "Absolute" or "God" "inaccurately." *Schelling's philosophisches System*, p. 114).

We spoke above of the "rest and inactivity" of the abstract identity or pure original unity; as pure unity the unconscious nature-mind is at rest. But as a composite unity it acts. The "absolute Reason," the "eternal Knowing" goes forth "out of the night of its essence" (W. I, 2, 66) and reveals itself for what it is, namely, a knowledge-*process*. Its "form" "in-forms" each moment of the world's development. This finite world in process is a "relative totality" or differentiated unity (S ≠ O). As a demiurge who stamps his image on all he fashions, each "form" partakes of both the "subjectivity" and the "objectivity," the "ideality" and "reality" of that "form of all forms" (Ib. 4, 327).

As examples of forms we may enumerate "plant," "beast" and "man." These are not essentially different and distinct; each is an embodiment of the one and same subject-objectivity that belongs to the universe. They are "universes"; or the "whole universe" is in "plant," "beast," "man"; or "plant" is the universe in the form of plant, "beast" the universe in the form of beast, "man" the universe in the form of man (Cf. W. I, 4, 394). "In God the conception of no individual thing is separated from the conception of all things" (Ib. 251). How then are the "forms" *different* from one another? Undifferentiated in "essence," in the many "forms" into which the "form of all forms" distinguishes itself there is a differentiated unity of "subjectivity" and "objectivity," there is a quantitative difference (quantitative only) of the ideal and the real constituents, each form embodies a plus or a minus of mind or of matter (Ib. 123). At its lowest stage the universe is matter, wherein the "objectivity" preponderates (S < O); at its highest stage it unveils itself in the philosophic mind and the artistic genius as truth and as beauty (Ib. 212; cf. 5, 284).

We have so far traced three unities eternally present in the universe as a structure of world-reason; for clarity's sake we have introduced simple symbols in parentheses and substituted consistent terminology, designating them as the pure original unity (S = S), the differentiated unity of the world in development (S ≠ O) wherein the "infinite and finite" are in "relative equality and opposition" (Ib. 4, 260), and the composite unity (S = O) where "infinite and finite are one" (Ib. 369). The movement from thesis to antithesis and from antithesis to synthesis, said Schelling earlier, is inwrought in the mechanism of the mind. They are present eternally in the unconscious universal mind; any act of its self-knowledge embraces them all together. The differentiated unity of the world in development is presented as a dialectic movement of the "three unities," which unities are "potencies" (Ib. 2, 66). This activity of nature's knowledge-process is a progressive "raising to a higher power," or, simply transliterating the mathematical term, "potentiating" of Reason. "All potencies," however, "are without any relation to time," "eternal" and "simultaneous" (Ib. 4, 135). Kuno Fischer remarks that between Schelling's "Method of Potentiation," Hegel's "Dialectic" and Schopenhauer's "Objectivization of the Will" there is "essential agreement," and that Schelling's method, coming to light in the year 1801, is prior.

The rational world-structure by which Schelling, in the terms of an "absolute Idealism" that makes the world development a knowledge-process and presents a synthesis of Spinoza and Plato is something more than a dark "night." His cherished figure for the Absolute is a lineal magnet. The magnet is one; it is none the less one if it has two poles, this, indeed, makes it two-in-one; and even if broken into fragments, each again is a magnet with its two poles again (W. I, 4, 137; 10). Moreover his images are full of color. The *pure original unity*, although a "subterranean God," is also "the eternal and invisible Father of all things" (Ib. 252). The *composite unity* is the miraculous light which illumines "that night," the "all-seeing eyes of the world, the source of all wisdom and knowledge" (Ib. 405); it is the "Son born to the Absolute, equally eternal with it, and of like essence" (Ib. 327). The *differentiated unity* is God incarnate, "subjected to the conditions of time" (Ib. 252; cf. 5, 294), and the various "forms" that belong to the differentiated unity are the "blessed first created beings which live immediately before the face of God" (Ib. 4, 405; 223). Not "black cows" as Hegel's caricature has it of Schelling's Absolute, but God, the eternal Son, the incarnate Son and the ministering angels!

Yet the old problem remains with us though its formulation is different. Earlier, the question "How does the Absolute go out of itself?" was "absolutely unanswerable." Now, it is meaningless to ask. It never does. "The fundamental error of all philosophy is the presupposition that the absolute identity has actually stepped out of itself" (W. I, 4, 119f). If we conceive *natura naturans* as a subject-object, it is "*itself* this eternal action" in which there is "no before nor after, no *transition* to action" (Ib. 2, 63).

Whence, then, nature's activity in space and time? Out

of the "conception" of "pure subject-object" (S = O), out of
the "idea" of "absolute knowing" outside of which, unlike
human selfconsciousness, "is nothing," we cannot draw the
differentiated unity (S ≠ O); we cannot say "*natura naturata*
is already outside of the Absolute" (W. I, 2, 67) unless it has
stepped out, as it were, *of its own accord.* If, in one place, it is
said that out of the "eternal self-knowledge" principles follow
"which are certain in themselves," whose self-evidence is the only
explanation there is of them (Ib. 70-1), it is said, in another place,
that the setting up of quantitative difference is, "from the standpoint of Reason," impossible (Ib. 4, 128). So important is this
differentiated unity that "the form of the subjectivity-objectivity
is not *actu* if a quantitative difference of the two is not set up"
(Ib. 124-5).

While he admits that "the actuality of the separated existence
lies only in itself," we have not yet seen how "the possibility
for it to be for itself is predetermined" in the higher unity as he
has defined it (W. I, 4, 282). To find the point of separation (to
pass from S = O to S ≠ O) is to him, as it was to Bruno, "nature's
deepest secret" (Ib. 328). Somehow the "relative totality" must
be given in the "absolute totality," the world in space and time
must be given in the Absolute, the "finite" must be given in the
"infinite." The "finite" is a succession in time, the "infinite"
is outside of all time; there is no causal relation between them
for causal relations belong only to that which is within time.
Whence then this "incarnation of God" in history? We bring
this wilfully labored questioning to an end by observing what we
find by way of answer. To account for the "finite" in time he
must speak of a "finite" before all time, of a "finite" that is
"timeless and infinite" (Ib. 248). Thus the existence of the
"finite" in time is attributed to the action of its own will before
all time (Ib. 250).

During Schelling's last period at Jena the word "God" is
often upon his lips. As we have seen, he refused to say without
qualification "God is the Universe" (or the pure Subject-Object,
the absolute Knowing, the universal Logos). Although he
equated "essence" and "form," by "God" he intends rather the
"divine essence" of *natura naturans.* As we may express it,

"God" is the pure, original unity of the unconscious World-Self. We observe here a significant change from the earlier standpoint. In our last two chapters the essence of the Absolute was an eternal activity, an energizing Will. But to define the "essence" of the Absolute of this chapter in terms of activity is to be "farthest from the idea of it"; the activity belongs to its "form," its composite unity. Though its hands are eternally busy, though its "Will" in the "timeless finite" (W. I, 4, 252) "in-forms" each moment in "ideality" and "reality" as the two activities we have throughout had with us molded the changing world, its heart is at "rest and inactivity."

The friendliness of Absolute Idealism to a religious world-view was recognized by Schelling at once and he announces a "new religion," the "absolute evangel" by which "heaven is truly won again" (W. I, 5, 120). Two lectures found a modern Philosophy of Religion. True theology, as indeed every other science, is neither simply empirical nor simply speculative. As empirical the business of theology is the historical construction of religions; to ignore this aspect is to turn theology into a mere matter of symbols, as in Kant. As speculative it recognizes the divine content, the "infinite" in the "finite," the "incarnation of God"; to ignore this aspect is to make all history unintelligible (Ib. 286-305).

Again, Absolute idealism is allied to a certain kind of Mysticism (similarly, after a century, in W. E. Hocking's *Meaning of God in Human Experience*). With regard to the pursuit of the sciences in general, "all knowledge is a strife for fellowship with the divine essence, a sharing in the same original Knowledge whose picture is the visible universe and whose birthplace is the source of eternal might" (W. I, 5, 218). The mystic, however, has gone beyond this strife to the identity that the strife presupposes. The "birthplace of the original Knowledge" is his own. He knows that "nature's deepest secret" is one with "the secret of the incarnation of God" (Ib. 290). He contemplates the "infinite in the finite" and sees their identity (Ib. 118-9).

The alliance, however, that receives more emphasis is that between Religion and Art. This has already become evident by the likeness of the mystic's insight just mentioned to that of the artist's genius mentioned earlier.   Schelling now raises his thought above any particular art product and considers art in the totality of all its expressions.   He grounds Aesthetics cosmologic- ally.   "The universe is in God as an absolute work of art and fashioned in eternal beauty" (W. I, 5, 385). A parallel seems to be suggested between "absolute Knowing" and "absolute Beauty" and to follow it we should have, over against the "absolute totality," a "relative totality," a progressive finite expression of the "absolute Beauty" in a succession of art forms.   Hence the blending of Art with Mythology.

Mythology is the production of the Divine Artist.   It devel- oped as speech developed.   "It is the necessary condition and the first material of all Art" (Ib. 405).   The "gods" of Mythology are the particularizations of "God," each is the "universe em- bodied in the particular" (Ib. 390).   There is thus revealed the necessity of Mythology to Religion; it is religion's "exoteric side" (Ib. 293), and, as Mythology is the expression of the "eternal Beauty," Religion and Art are mutually interrelated. "The inner bond that unites Art and Religion—the complete impossibility, on the one hand, to give to Art a poetic world except within and through Religion, and, on the other hand, to bring Religion to true objective appearing except through Art— raises to a necessity the scientific knowledge of Art on the part of the genuinely pious man" (Ib. 352).

Schelling's lectures on Art from which we have quoted and which were first published after his death, were delivered also at Würzburg.   His final paper on the Philosophy of Art was read at Munich before a select audience including the crown prince on the king's birthday in the year 1807.   It contains "the most beau- tiful exhibition of poetic prose in the German tongue" (Kinkel). Art, he says, is not to be a slavish copying of nature, nor is it to be an idealization of nature, as though "truth, beauty and good- ness" were not "the actual."   The true artist expresses what is the fundamental principle for every inspired investigator of nature, "the holy, eternal, creative original force of the world which produces all things out of itself" (W. I, 7, 293).   Greek Mythology gave its gods to Greek sculpture (Ib. 316); similarly, Christian Mythology has provided subjects for the painting of a

Michael Angelo or a Raphael, their art revealing, better than the Greek, man's susceptibility to higher influences (Ib. 317).

Schelling's contributions to the Philosophy of Nature after leaving Jena also extend to 1807, and offer rather a Religion of Nature. The three stages of nature he designates as matter, light and life, using the symbols A^1, A^2 and A^3 (W. I, 7, 184), and it is upon the relation of the first named to the Absolute that his thought lingers. He will have neither an "inconceivable creation" (Ib. 2, 378), nor an "architect of the world" as though matter were originally outside of the Absolute (Ib. 360; 7, 192), nor an "original that propagates itself through successive generations" which would mean the abolition of absoluteness (Ib. 7, 191; 6, 35-6). Creationism, dualism and emanationism are all excluded. We may thus trace Schelling's writings on the Philosophy of Nature to their end, remarking only their recurrent refrain: "The One in All can be recognized in every part of matter; everything lives only in God" (Ib. 2, 376). "The existence of God is an empirical truth, the ground of all experience. To him who has inwardly grasped this is the door to the Philosophy of Nature open," he can live "the real life of the spirit in and with nature" (Ib. 7, 246-7). "The re-birth of sciences and all education can only begin from the recognition of the All and its eternal Unity" (Ib. 141).

V

THE WORLD-SELF'S UNITY (continued)

(*Würzburg, 1803-1806*)

Our every-day phrase "Love me love my dog" applied in full
force to Schelling. Not to agree with him or failure to recognize
his genius was all too often to be the victim of his abuse. In 1800
he was sued for defamation by the editor of the *Literary Times* of
Jena. He issued a counter-suit and both parties were fined.
After two years the controversy was renewed and Schelling's intention to leave Jena was strengthened. His last lectures there were
delivered in the spring of 1803. In May the friendly arrange-
ment between Caroline and her husband for a divorce became
effective and her marriage with Schelling was performed by his
father at Murrhardt. Here the latter occupied the position which
Oetinger had held at the time of his death in 1782. Oetinger,
while a student at Tübingen, had discovered the writings of
Jakob Böhme (1575-1624) and was ever afterwards Böhme's
enthusiastic disciple. While at his father's home Schelling con-
versed much of Oetinger and Böhme with Pregizer, a follower
of Oetinger, who found in Schelling a "pleasing echo" of the
"two genuinely enlightened witnesses and heralds of the divine
truth" (L. II, 179).

In the autumn Schelling was appointed by the Bavarian government to the position of Professor of the Philosophy of Nature
at Würzburg, where, through the changes effected by the Peace
of Lüneville, protestants were admitted to public office. Following Austerlitz however, the Peace of Pressburg caused Würzburg
to fall again under the rule of an Austrian. Schelling wished to
retain his connections with the Bavarian government and his
Würzburg period ended in the spring of 1806 when he left for
Munich.

His lectures at Würzburg were to a large extent an exposition
of his system and its historical significance and they were ac-
commodated to the needs of his numerous students. Upon the

death of Kant he penned a memorial to the immortal genius: "The fires of further progress have only served to separate the pure gold of his philosophy from its ephemeral alloy, and to reveal it in its unsullied lustre" (W. I, 6, 3). His most significant writing, "Philosophy and Religion" (1804), develops elements of his teaching more fully than previously and serves to estrange further former adherents. His friend Eschenmayer, whose coöperation he had desired in founding the "Journal for Speculative Physics" (1800-02) had, by his "Philosophy in its Transition to Non-Philosophy" (1803), challenged the comprehensiveness of Schelling's system.

The "non-Philosophy" suggested as a completion of "Philosophy" was Religion; Eschenmayer "would supplement philosophy by faith" (W. I, 6, 13). He regards "faith" as an advance upon philosophical thinking. In reply Schelling cements the bond between philosophy and religion and shows that the God of Religion, with whom he equates the Absolute of Philosophy, is an object, not of a kind of religious intuition inaccessible to philosophical perception, but of immediate knowledge.

Schelling affirms that no "mediated" knowledge or state of mind that is mediated by conditioned knowledge can apprehend or be the ground of apprehending anything that we mean by the term "God." This state of mind, whether called "faith," "presentiment," "religious intuition," "devotion," "feeling," or "by any other name," is inferior to "rational knowledge." The "Dogmatism" of the contested view can offer a type of knowledge that is applicable merely to empirical objects, to finite things; of the things of the reason and of the supersensible world it is a merely external spectator, or, rather, no spectator at all. This knowledge, mediated by the experience of the finite, has faith for its antithesis. The more the negativity of knowledge is recognized the more valuable faith becomes and the more philosophy must surrender what is essentially philosophical (W. I, 6, 17). The philosopher would be permitted a speculative knowledge concerning the experience on account of which he is to pass on to faith; but he is in a sorry plight if, through knowing and in knowing, he has not a clearer knowledge than that which proceeds out of "faith."

Such is the opponent's flight. "What positive ground he cites for the grounding of his faith cannot yield the evidence, since, if faith could be proved, it would cease to be faith" (Ib. 18). The positive ground for faith is the negativity of knowledge! All attempts which limit the evidence that lies in the idea of the Absolute and lead it back to some "faith" or what-not in an individual, must be considered as wholly inadequate; they not only do not present the evidence required but destroy its very essence (Ib. 27).

This plight is made worse by turning to the object of such faith. "Conditioned knowledge" can only give a "not-Absolute" (Ib. 21). If there were merely a mediated knowledge of the Absolute, whatever the means of mediation, the Absolute would become only something assumed in order to philosophize. The mind which does not possess the "true rational knowledge" is left with subjective gropings; it cannot establish the existential reality of its object, it possesses no conception that at the same time sets up an existence. The God who is merely an object of faith, so far from being an actual expression of the divine nature, becomes a mere *numen;* in all dogmatic systems the "In-itself" becomes but a product of the soul and thus ceases to be "in-itself" (Ib. 27).

Every man, discontented with the finite, is by nature driven to seek an absolute. In trying to find it by means of reflection he finds it vanishes. By luck, illumination or revelation an unexpected harmony may enter the soul which, in its thrill of unexpectedness, may have the advantage over the rational knowledge that knows no yearning. But scarcely is the harmony established when reflection enters and the unexpected guest has gone. Religion in this ephemeral form is a mere appearing of God in the soul inasmuch as the soul is still in the sphere of reflection and at a state of variance. So far from being an actual elevation and higher power, this "faith" or "presentiment" is to realize all its worth in but a limited sphere; at best it is but "a particular aspect of that general relation to the Absolute which exists in its most complete form in the knowledge through reason" (W. I, 6, 19). We turn therefore from the "dogmatism of religion" and the "non-philosophy of faith" to vindicate "reason and philosophy" (Ib. 20).

In equating God with the Absolute he is replying to those who would make the God of Religion an infinitely higher power of the Absolute than is the Absolute of Philosophy. But there can be no "empty space" outside of the Absolute to be filled by faith. By the Absolute is meant that which excludes all limitation. As we are not dealing here with "generic notions," "the Absolute cannot be distinguished from the Absolute, the Eternal from the Eternal" (W. I, 6, 21). So far from there being no knowledge of the Absolute the knowledge of the Absolute is more direct and intimate than any other knowledge. "We have in Reason an absolute affirmation, that is, an immediate knowledge of the idea of God"; in fact, "God or the Absolute is the only immediate object of knowledge" (Ib. 151). Our knowledge of God is "speculative," "truly rational," "unconditioned" and "embraces the universe" (Ib. 18-27).

Many words can add but little to a positive description of what is meant by "immediate knowledge" and its "idea of the Absolute"; "to describe the evidence which lies in the idea of the Absolute human speech is too weak" (Ib. 27). The idea of the Absolute cannot be attained by following the philosopher's description of it for descriptions are only of what it is not, and, as merely negative, they never bring the Absolute itself in its true nature before the soul. Descriptions can offer only a conditioned knowledge of the Absolute, and "a conditioned knowledge of an unconditioned is impossible" (Ib. 21). Again, to describe the Absolute merely as the identity of all opposites is but a negative description; the philosopher does not take "the ideal or subjective in one hand and the real or objective in the other" and put them together; the Absolute is not a manufactured product (Ib. 22).

The kind of knowledge the soul has of the Absolute does not come through instruction. Descriptions and conceptions of reflection at best but show the negativity of all finite antitheses and lead the soul to the perception of the infinite only indirectly. The intention of Philosophy is not so much to give something to a man but to separate him as completely as possible from the accidental which the body, the phenomenal world and the sensuous life has brought to him, and to lead him back to the Original. This "simple" is perceived by an individual but is universally valid; it is the light of all our seeing. The kind of knowledge is just as absolute as the Absolute itself, it is the true substance and eternal part of the soul. The essence of the soul is one with God. The "truth and evidence" are "evident of themselves" and must therefore be absolute, must be God's own nature itself (Ib. 26-7).

We observed earlier that the Absolute of the Philosophy of Nature and the Absolute of the Transcendental Philosophy took the same name in the Absolute Idealism. The most common appellation for the Absolute is now the more emotional term "God." The following may serve as an expression characteristic of his Würzburg lectures that establish the basis for his Philosophy of Nature: "God is immediately, in virtue of the self-affirmation of his idea, absolute-All, and the absolute-All is nothing other than the self-affirmation of God" (W. I, 6, 174).

Again, with regard to our "immediate knowledge" of this Absolute, a former quotation may be recalled: "There is not an absolute knowledge and outside of this still an Absolute, but both are one." Our absolute knowledge is the Absolute's knowledge; or, to express as simply as we know how what is meant by that "immediate relation to the Absolute, available only to the essence of the soul which is one with the Absolute and which is the Absolute itself" (W. I, 6, 23), in the phrase "the idea of the Absolute," the genitive ("of the Absolute") is both a subjective and an objective genitive. The "idea of the Absolute" is at once the Absolute's idea and our idea of the Absolute. The "knowledge of God" means God's knowledge and our knowledge of God in a pure original unity. The Absolute (or God) is the pure original unity which becomes separated by reflection into the subjective and the objective, the ideal and the real. Originally, the "absolutely-Ideal" is in itself the "absolutely-Real" (Ib. 25). "The nature of God is absolute-Ideality which, as such, is absolute-Reality" (Ib. 26).

With regard to the theological result of this view it would end the Dilemma of God:

I am that I am, how well indeed I know it,
But men say not "He is," they must then me intuit.
I am now the thoughts of men, my knowledge now is theirs,
But then I know not that I am, I am only in mine heirs.

Schelling has solved the dilemma by making God both my knowledge and his knowledge. On the one hand, to speak of the existence of God and to affirm that he is outside of and independent of all our knowledge is to speak in a manner than has no meaning. A god who is said to be only an absolute object cannot be an object at all in any meaningful sense of the word. It is absurd to speak of knowing the existence of an object that cannot be known. Kant introduced an epoch of religious "faith" in such an object, and in all "dogmatic" systems, Spinozism, Criticism and Fichteanism, the reality of the Absolute is spoken of as "outside of and independent of ideality" (W. I, 6, 17; 27). Even if knowledge were to be actually and completely extinguished "in the Absolute," no "faith" could bring us anything more complete than what was already contained in the knowledge that is extinguished (Ib. 19). On the other hand, to take the idea of God as merely subjective, as a mediated knowledge, is equally false. Where the "conception" is not adequate to the "existence" we have only a "not-Absolute"; where the reality does not follow out of the thinking, where to the conception something must be added by which existence is to be set up the conception is only of a conditioned, not of the unconditioned (Ib. 22.)

When the "immediate knowledge" becomes a theme for reflection, it can best be set forth in the form of a disjunctive proposition: it is *both* ideal *and* real. This is the form used by philosophy in its Ontological Argument for the existence of God. Its inventors did not mean that God is a compounding of the ideal and the real, but that God, as the absolutely ideal, is *as such* also absolutely real (Ib. 25). This result means that not only is the Ontological Argument the *only* argument for the existence of God, but that its validity involves the pre-acceptance of Absolute Idealism.

"One may say a hundred times and yet a hundred times that

for us there is no subjective and objective and that the Absolute is to us only the *absolute* identity of the two, but still they do not understand" (W. I, 6, 22). For our own part we have tried to understand and find ourselves at the pinnacle of thought to which former designations of the Absolute have been leading. Designated in the Transcendental Philosophy as "absolute I," "absolute Will" and "absolute Selfconsciousness," or in the Philosophy of Nature as "World-Soul" and "absolute Productivity," and now, in the System of Identity as "absolute Reason," "absolute Knowing" or simply as the "Absolute" or "God," the primal unity has been the principle of all his philosophizing and has always been claimed as the only principle on which philosophy is possible. "All philosophy begins and has begun with the idea of the Absolute quickened into life" (Ib. 27). Its nature has now become clear. This unity is a universal (unconscious) Intelligence, which, in human intelligences, perceives its activity in its action. The unity embraces at once ideality and reality; it is an intelligence which is at once both knowledge and existence. Man's immediate knowledge of it, the "origin of which knowledge is the origin of philosophy itself," has left all finite knowledge behind, it is God's knowledge of himself, it is God. "Yet still they do not understand!"

Schelling now faces squarely the problem of the origin of the differentiated unity out of the composite unity, of the world outside of God out of the world in God. Let us distinguish them again. On the one hand we have the universe in the absolute totality which "God is immediately in virtue of the self-affirmation of his idea," the "self-objectivization" of God, the "pure *natura naturans*." As only "ideality" God could not be; this eternal world is his "reality," his "counterpart," the existence implied in the conception; it is the timeless process of his self-revelation, his eternal "subject-objectivization," the "transcendental theogony"; it is the Platonic "world of ideas."

On the other hand, in contrast to this closed whole, we have the differentiated unity of the world outside of God, the world of finite ideas with their apparently metaphysical independence, the world of matter or of this plant, this animal, this man. This is the world of empirical ideas; in this world the existence or reality of anything is not implied merely in its conception or ideality. It is the world in space and time, "*natura naturata*" in an endless causal nexus, each thing being determined by another thing. It is the world of quantitative difference in which there is evil and only relative good.

Let us now name these the Eternal World $(S = O)$ and the temporal world $(S \neq O)$, so that the problem now becomes: How comes the temporal world to "fall away" from the Eternal World, how can philosophy account for this apostasy? The situation is such that, since there is no fundamental dualism, the Eternal World cannot itself be responsible for the "falling away," and yet the "falling away" must somehow take place within it; and, on the other hand, with emanation excluded, with the Absolute never "going out of itself," the temporal world itself must be responsible for the apostasy.

Since the "possibility" for the origin of the temporal world has been distinguished from its "actuality" we ask then, in the first place, how is the "leap" a "possibility"? "The ground of the possibility of the falling away" lies in the Eternal World's "freedom" (W. I, 6, 40). The Eternal World is, in one aspect, *not* free. Since God as mere "essence" or "ideality" could not be, but must have "form" or "reality," which "reality" is just this Eternal World, then the Eternal World is absolutely necessary. Yet at the same time, in another aspect, it *is* free. The composite unity is the "form" of which the pure unity is the "essence." It is not only the "reality" which it is as the counterpart of the "ideality," but, as we have seen earlier, it is itself a perfect equilibrium of "ideality" and "reality." As "another Absolute" it has "existence in itself," or a relation to itself such as it has to God. "Along with the essence of itself the Absolute bestows upon its counterpart independence also. This in-itself-ness is freedom" (Ib. 39).

Thus, on the one hand, the Eternal World is necessary to give God reality, and, on the other hand, to be a true "counterpart" it must have "the complete possibility of its existence in itself." This freedom of the Eternal World or composite unity is the freedom of perfect equilibrium. Herein, then, lies the possibility for the origin of the temporal world. The freedom of the

Eternal World is absolute, it is freedom without any bias. It may thus act "according to its egoity," that is, it may "fall away from God" and become the differentiated unity of the temporal world. Hence, on the one hand, God has no responsibility for the apostasy, and, on the other hand, the possibility for the existence of the temporal world lies outside of the temporal world.

The possibility for the fall into finiteness being thus established, we have now to ask in the second place: What of its actuality, how is this to be explained? "The ground of the *actuality*," Schelling replies, "lies in that which has fallen away," the temporal world is produced "only through and for itself" (W. I, 6, 40; 29); by which he means that it is completely impossible to explain the origin of finite ideas of finite things directly out of the infinite composite unity. Though finite things exist, no genetic explanation of them is possible: "the falling away cannot be *explained*" (Ib. 42). And this for the simple reason that it took place "outside of all time" (Ib. 41; it is a "*That-handlung*" and not a "*Thatsache*"). We cannot, therefore, apply to it such explanations as are applicable to transitions in the temporal world with their causal linkage. It is enough that its possibility has been demonstrated. The falling away is an expression of the potentiality which is involved in the idea of absolute freedom.

As always hitherto, Schelling now turns his attention from the Absolute that stands at the beginning to the Absolute that is to be achieved at the "end" of an infinite progress, to the finite's teleological Absolute. (That Bréhier, "*Les Grands Philosophes, Schelling*," p. 177, and Braun, "*Hinauf zum Idealismus! Schelling-Studien*," p. 142, speak of the Absolute as a "paradise to be regained" as a new thought to Schelling in 1804 is unaccountable.) The perfect equilibrium of the Eternal World has been disturbed; the possibility of the exercise of its freedom has been (inexplicably) actualized; the result is the finite world. In that very disturbance of the perfect equilibrium, however, a return to it is involved; the unrest of the finite world "intends" the rest of the infinite world. "The great intention of the universe and its history is nothing other than the restoration, the perfect reconciliation with absoluteness" (W. I, 6, 42). The finite is at present suffering from the "guilt" of the "Fall"; but, through the "purification" and that "true morality" which exists in knowing the infinite, it can be healed. The "centrifugal" tendency of the "egoity," or "as it were, the Iliad," is counter-balanced by the "centripetal" tendency, the "Odyssey," of the return home to God (Ib. 57). Immortality is the life in which the individual has finally freed himself from finite desire and the finite existence that is his "punishment," the eternal and blessed life in which he loses his individuality (Ib. 61).

By the foregoing Schelling has met the charge that speculative knowledge is inferior to religious "faith" and that there must be a "transition from philosophy to non-philosophy." His natural-istic disciples who are "incapable of comprehending the essential mysteries of science" are treated with contempt (W. I, 6, 15); his true followers will recognize that Religion and Absolute Idealism have a sanctuary in common. If there is a knowledge of God both philosophy and religion may stand; if there is not, they fall together. Historically they were found united in the Greek Mysteries with their insight into the "great topics for the sake of which alone it is worth while to philosophize" (Ib. 16). These great topics are such as we have dealt with: the origin of things, the original innocence, the fall, its punishment and the purification therefrom. Religion must retain these higher esoteric truths and philosophy will remain joined with it "in an eternal bond" (Ib. 70).

VI

TRANSCENDENT AND IMMANENT WILL

(Munich, 1806-1820; Erlangen, 1820-1827)

In Munich Schelling was made a member of the Academy of Science upon its reorganization in 1807, and appointed as General Secretary to the newly founded Academy of Fine Arts, which position he held until 1823. Upon the founding of the new Order for the recognition of public merit he was among the first to be knighted. During his last days at Würzburg he expressed his dissatisfaction with doing anything by halves, and has come to see that it is "religion, the public faith, the life in the state" which is the fulcrum upon which to rest the lever to "shake this dead humanity" (L. II, 78), but at Munich, without the office of lecturer, he was left to develop his thoughts in private.

His work on "Human Freedom" (1809) faced the problem of explaining the possibility of evil in terms of his absolute monism; his private and unpublished lectures at Stuttgart (1810) present his System of Identity as a doctrine of God; and his reply to an attack by Jacobi, the president of the Academy of Science, who, regarding philosophy as inadequate to explain the problems of freedom and God, demanded a dualism between the natural and the supernatural, lashes his opponent for an "intentionally deceptive accusation of Atheism" (1811). To the more friendly criticisms of Eschenmayer, who now objects to the "anthropomorphic" nature of Schelling's God, Schelling replies in 1812.

Baader, a fellow member of the Academy and another disciple of Böhme, occasioned Schelling to write to his father in 1806 for some works by Oetinger (L. II, 101) and three years later Schelling has written to Pregizer that "the time is near in which that which was seen by Oetinger is to be perceived more universally, vividly and definitely" (Ib. 179).

To include in our references the whole of Schelling's productions during the twenty-one years of this period there only remain to be mentioned his address upon the "Deities of Samothrace"

(1815), his dialogue concerning death and immortality entitled "The Connection of Nature with the Spirit-World," his honorary lectures in 1821-1823 while on furlough at Erlangen upon the history of modern philosophy and the philosophy of mythology, and, finally, a section of an uncompleted work, "The Ages of the World." The dialogue and the lectures remained unpublished. With regard to "The Ages of the World," although he never completed more than a third of this projected work, he promised the whole of it to his friends several times from 1811 to 1821, and advertised it to the public in 1815! (Kuno Fischer: *Schelling*, p. 163f.)

With whatever zeal for intellectual reform he anticipated his work in Munich, when Caroline died in 1809 it seemed as though the last bond that held him to this world was cut (L. II, 187), and though a second marriage in 1812 brought him domestic happiness, his desire to remain hidden (Ib. 248) was only fitfully disturbed by thoughts of the world's need for his ideas, which thoughts, however, were accompanied by misgivings as to his ability to express his philosophy as fully and completely as he would like (Ib. 429). When a call to Tübingen was in question, he agreed with the king that "his philosophy would never make peace with the Tübingen theologians"; "to prove the existence of God out of miracles and prophecies as external facts is that crassest Judaism against which Christ himself had to contend with in the Pharisees and lawyers" (Ib. 278-280).

Invited in 1816 to become head of the faculty of philosophy in Jena, he felt himself attracted by the offer, not by the prospect of becoming again "merely a teacher of philosophy," but by the opportunity he could provide for himself there to make "a gradual and historical transition to Theology, and thus, under divine blessing, do something distinctive for all Germany" (L. II, 366). But his Bavarian connections held him in Munich.

In facing the fact of evil, Schelling does not soften the problem by making evil merely the absence of good. We have seen that all our finite ideas of finite existences were attributed to a falling away from the Absolute, to the finite's actualization of what, within the infinite, was a possibility. This made all finite existence estrangement from God and attributable to a non-temporal act of freedom exercised egoistically. The misuse of the freedom was *groundless*.

With regard to evil, although it can rise only in a finite personality such as man, it is not man's individuality in itself that casts the veil of melancholy over all existence (W. I, 7, 399); active egoity is, in fact, necessary to give life its keenness (Ib. 400). To make evil arise out of mere limitation, shortcoming or deprivation, or out of the natural condition of animality is to miss completely its essential nature (Ib. 368). Evil must have "something positive" in it (Ib. 371; 354). This positive character of evil reveals itself in man who, as the battle-ground of cosmic forces, has inverted their true relation, and its essence is best understood as the complete rending free of the blind, individual will from the luminous, universal Will (Ib. 364-5; 395; 400). Evil is neither the work of nature nor the will of God (Ib. 401); it is an act of man's freedom. But if all things are immanent in God, if the individual will is immanent in the universal Will, how is this freedom possible? Can man's misuse of freedom be *grounded?*

A. We shall not trace in detail his treatment of this problem but present his view of God as applied to it. It is unequivocally in terms of Will that his Absolute is here defined and the connection with freedom is at hand. Only God is unconditioned, and to be unconditioned is to be free. Mistaken Pantheism may teach blind necessity, but correctly, so far from immanence in God being contradictory to freedom, "that which is not free is necessarily outside of God" (W. I, 7, 347). "Freedom is the positive conception of the in-itself in general" (Ib. 352). "In the final analysis, there is no other existence except Will. Will is original Being and all the predicates of original Being —groundlessness, independence of time, self-affirmation—are applicable only to Will" (Ib. 350).

It is in the highest stage of nature that it becomes evident that the original, uncaused or groundless existence is Will (Ib.). With the pattern of our previous presentation in mind, we speak first of the pure original unity (now termed "indifference"; contrast pp. 25 and 39 above) which stands prior to that becoming. In doing so we are at once at "the supreme point of the whole enquiry." This original unity, the "absolute indifference," "original Ground, or, rather, the Unground" is the *prius* of all difference. It is before the opposites; in it the opposites are indistinguishable yet implicit (Ib. 406). It is not *both* this *and* that; it is *neither* this *nor* that; and it is needed to give meaningfulness to any duality for "without an Unground there is no duplexity of principles" (Ib. 407). In this eternal beginning of the divine revelation the divine life rests inactive. In this aspect God is not love for love's mystery involves deliberate union of independents (Ib. 408). Nor is he personality, for personality involves consciousness and achieved unity (Ib. 412). "But then," Schelling adds, "is the starting point the whole?"

B. The original unity, "the Unground, divides itself into two equally eternal beginnings" (W. I, 7, 408). Thus out of the unity yonside of consciousness a duality arises and God is on his way. The opposites are variously designated. His leading designation reminds us of the distinction theological speculation has made in speaking of God as *causa sui*. We have thus, on the one hand, the notion of God's existence, and, on the other hand, the notion of the cause of his existence, and, since God is the cause of himself, there must be that in God, viz. the cause of God, which is not God himself. "Since there is nothing before or outside of God," says Schelling, "he must therefore have the ground of his existence in himself" (Ib. 357). There is that "in God which is not God himself," "that which is the ground of his existence" (Ib. 359); "neither is the other, nor is either without the other." The relation between these two principles is not temporal for they mutually presuppose each other; both are equally eternal.

This ground of God's existence is now made something "real and actual." It is "nature" (Ib. 358). God is not merely the perfect world-order of the abstract idealists whose philosophy is a disembodied spirit. "Nature in God" provides a living Realism as a basis for true Idealism. "All things have their ground in that which is the ground of God's existence," and, since this ground of God's existence is that in God which is not God, they are just as much inseparable from God as they are distinguishable from him.

"The first beginning of creation is the longing of the one to produce itself, or the will of the ground" (W. I, 7, 395), a longing which is equally eternal as the eternal One himself (Ib. 359). As the human mind knows a state of nameless longing for some unknown good, or feels a chaotic mass of thoughts not yet reduced to order, so the "ground of God's existence" or "nature in God" is a chaos of forces and a divine impulse for revelation. The reciprocal opposites are now this vague longing and that condition of illumination by the understanding for which the desire of the ground longs. On the one hand stands the "dark will," the unintelligible principle of things, the "inconceivable basis of reality"; on the other hand is the "understanding," the "will in the will," the "word of that longing," "an inner reflexive representation in God himself by means of which he sees himself in his likeness," a representation or idea which is "in the beginning with God" and is "God himself begotten in God" (Ib. 359-361).

The two principles enunciated bear a likeness to the two activities of our second chapter. The nameless longing of the ground's will resembles the limitless, expansive force; the understanding, in providing limits to the vague will is analogous to the limiting, restrictive force. As Schelling now conceives these principles he presents what came to be considered as a synthesis of Hegel and Schopenhauer. "As Hegel constructed one-sidedly upon the logical, ideal principle, and Schopenhauer predominantly upon the illogical, real principle of the will, so Schelling's later standpoint offers the possibility of a re-union of these antithetical systems, whose principles he himself had furnished" (von Hartmann).

Since all is Will, the opposites are also presented characteristically as two divine wills, or, rather, as two directions of the one Will. (1) On the one hand is the real principle, the "will of the ground." It is not conscious will, and at the same time not completely unconscious, that is, it does not move according to blind mechanical necessity but as nature striving to unfold itself involuntarily and purposively. (2) On the other hand is the ideal principle, the "universal Will," the "will to revelation," the "will to love by which the word is expressed in nature and through which God first makes himself personal" (W. I, 7, 395).

The opposition of principles thus expressed changes their order, putting the restrictive principle first, and makes the opposition not one that exists between the two principles in "that which in God is not God", but one that exists between "that which in God is not God" on the one side and "God himself" on the other. The difficulties provided by Schelling's changing vocabulary is enhanced by the difficulty that must ever inhere in an enquiry into eternal, unconscious origins, as for example, to choose a fitting analogy, into the passage from non-consciousness to consciousness of an intuition of artistic genius.

C. In so far as the condition of duality or antithesis is necessary to the progressive divine revelation, at any moment in the course of nature and human history the two opposites would be united in a unity that is not a perfect equilibrium and thus correspond to what we have termed throughout the differentiated unity. If, however, we now consider the eternal unity which is the togetherness of the opposites yet unopposed in the pure original unity, and which again binds together the opposites within the differentiated unity and gives unity to the process, this eternal and living unity appears as a perfect equilibrium, or what we have termed the composite unity, of ground and existence, of real and ideal, of nature and spirit. The result is an interesting synthesis of Pantheism and Theism. God is not mere nature, for "nature in God" is but the "ground of his existence." He is the composite unity embracing in one both the ground of existence and the existing itself. Thus, as in Pantheism, all things are immanent in God, and as in Theism, God is Mind, for it is in mind "that the ground for existence is one with the existing," that both are "actual at the same time"; "mind is the absolute identity of the two" (W. I, 7, 408).

There is thus set up a conception of God according to which he is personal. The bond of personality is mind (Ib. 414), and that God is "mind" we have just seen. The "binding" that is involved in the meaning of personality is the union of an independent with a basis independent of it (Ib. 394), the conscious and living union of the ideal and real. This union God now is. Therefore God, "through the union in him of the ideal principle with the independent ground that is relative to this

ideal principle, since basis and existing are necessarily joined
in him in one absolute existence, is the highest personality"
(Ib. 395). To both Fichte and Spinoza God had to remain
impersonal because the former conceived him without nature and
the latter only as nature (Ib.). For his own view Schelling claims
originality (Ib. 412).

Since God is personal in the sense defined, nature's necessity
is not impersonal. Nature is to be explained dynamically and
its laws reduced to Will. "God is a life" and the divine necessity
is personal and ethical. The Leibnitzian assumption of a plurality of possible worlds can now have no place, nor can the Spinozistic assumption of inviolable necessity (W. I, 7, 395-6).

It cannot be said that Schelling has here suddenly found an
"irrational" in the "Absolute." Those who assert it should
give volume and page. That the process of the finite world
with its "irrationalities" is "in God" as well as "not God"
is another way of expressing what has been expressed earlier.
The irrational and contingent is in the formation of things,
"especially of the organic" (W. I, 7, 376). The new and obscure
phraseology borrowed from medieval mysticism and the pro-
miscuous use of the term "God" have not brought conceptions
that are essentially new. He emphasizes his old thought of the
Absolute as Will. The composite and the differentiated aspects
of the divine unity are interwoven in a dynamic process. The
composite unity is emphasized as a nexus. "God," as the composite unity of the real and ideal, maintains an equilibrium in the
process of nature and history considered as a whole. How else
can immanent Will be defined except as that which maintains
its pursuit consistently within a process of which no moment
is its complete realization, of which, in fact, each moment is a
differentiated unity of the Will that is being defined and the will
that is opposed to it? This appears to be the thought obfuscated
by Schelling's difficult presentation and which we elaborate
further in section C below.

D. We left unanswered the question of human freedom which
is the subject of the treatise under consideration, and now
answer it briefly. We have to distinguish between the possibility of evil and its actuality. As to its possibility, it was

with a view to explaining evil that Schelling enlarged upon the conception of the "ground of God." Evil finds its ultimate explanation in that in God which is not God. Evil comes into existence only after that stage is reached in which God realizes himself as Mind. This he does in the human mind; here God exists "as *actu*" (W. I, 7, 364). In Man, indeed, we recognize again the pure original unity which Schelling has writ large as the cosmological Absolute. "Man is set on that summit where he has in himself the authority of self-motion to good and evil. The bond of the principles in him is not necessity but freedom. He stands at the point of decision" (Ib. 374). Evil is only possible in an individual will which can rend itself free from the universal Will of Love and follow the impulse of the dark, natural, particular will (of the ground).

As to its actuality, this is due to an act that takes place yonside of consciousness, outside of time and "in the beginning of creation." In each consciousness there remains a trace of it. A man feels somehow that what he is he is by necessity: "As things are I am as I am." He feels also in some way responsible and blameworthy for what he is. These intimations of necessity and freedom within us are conscious traces of our pre-conscious choice of evil, of an unconscious act which was both free and necessary, of an act which was not temporal and empirical but "intelligible." Though this "intelligible act" cannot come forth in consciousness, all consciousness presupposes existence, and this existence is the original Will that is the basis of consciousness. The necessity of the intelligible act is "an inner necessity arising out of the nature of action itself"; it is not determined by anything outside of it but by the definite character of the particular individual, by his inmost nature. According to his inmost nature man is free, for that is free which acts, not according to caprice, but according to the laws of its own nature. Thus both deterministic and indeterministic accounts of evil are rejected and the choice of evil is both necessary and free.

The non-relatedness of this intelligible act reminds us of his account of the actualization of the finite when it "fell away" from the infinite. It stands within no causal or temporal relations. That falling away of the intelligible world (that "*That-*

handlung") into the actual spacial-temporal world was confessedly inexplicable. Schelling has now given his explanation of the actuality of evil; when, however, he makes the empirical character of the individual depend upon his intelligible act which is "eternal" in the sense that it took place in the beginning of creation, the act must be that of a prototypical Man who is both all of us and none of us. "Man," he says, "has from eternity attached himself to egotism and self-seeking, and all who are born, are born under the influence of the dark principle of evil" (W. I, 7, 380).

E. Thus Man at the beginning of history, having passed from being the pure unity of an absolute I (to introduce fittingly an expression long since left behind) into the differentiated unity of an empirical I, has the whole of history in which to return to the Absolute. The end of human history is a condition of "absoluteness" in which the opposites become indistinguishably one again. This final goal at which the process of God's revelation aims is his complete actualization, the distant future time of which the Scriptures speak when "God will be all in all" (W. I, 7, 404).

God as final goal is "absolute personality." "Above mind is the initial Unground which is no longer indifference" (i. e., no longer the original undifferentiated unity), "nor any longer the identity of the two principles" (i. e., the composite unity), "but which is the universal unity affecting everything equally yet affected by nothing, permeating all beneficently yet independent of all—in a word, Love, which is all in all" (Ib. 408). When Will is completely realized it can no longer be termed will, and "Love" defines the oppositionless unity attained after separation and conflict.

After the work on human freedom followed the productions mentioned at the beginning of this chapter. We have systematized our presentation in five lettered divisions, and now link his development to the end of this period with the foregoing by following the same outline to the end of our chapter.

A. "The original essence" is the "absolute identity of the real and ideal" but only "in itself," that is, as having not yet revealed itself as such (W. I, 7, 424). If "A = A" (i. e., the subject-A linked with the object-A; S = O) represents the identity that has revealed itself, or the "essence in the absolute form," we are here dealing with only the "A" or "A°" (i. e., the subject that is just subject; S = S), or the "essence in itself" (Ib. 426). It is the Unconscious of God in which he has the two principles in himself without setting himself up as the one or the other (Ib. 434). The "essence of the absolute identity" is the God that is posited as Alpha, but, as Alpha, he is only *Deus implicitus* or the unevolved God; or rather since the name of God is used less exactly when designating an unconscious intelligence, Schelling now says it is that which is not as yet, but which comes to transfigure itself into, the personal God (Ib. 8, 81). This "one original essence" that stands prior to the unfolding into opposition is, therefore, called simply "the Absolute" (Ib. 165).

What is the first principle of Philosophy? "As the supreme proposition Descartes had '*Cogito ergo sum*,' Fichte 'I am I,' but in a living system which is a sequence, not of propositions, but of the moments of a progress and evolution, we cannot speak of this kind of supreme proposition" (W. I, 9, 216). Spinoza taught us to raise ourselves up to the infinite, but "how deep he sank down again when he made this infinite a Substance, i. e., something dead and motionless, and when he explained this Substance as a unity of extension and thinking— the two weights, as it were, by which he draws it right down again into the sphere of the finite!" (Ib. 218).

To surpass these attempts and to improve upon all one-sided systems the basis of his own philosophy is the absolute Subject. Since definitions always de-limit, "the absolute Subject is indefinable, incomprehensible, infinite" (W. I, 9, 219). These terms, however, define what it is not. Conceived affirmatively "it is itself nothing other than the eternal Freedom"; "it is pure Will itself," the "Will in so far as it neither wills nor does not will, but is in complete equipoise" (Ib. 220). Though a systematic exposition makes it necessary to connect this "absolute Subject" or "eternal Freedom" with the pure initial unity, when he adds that this Will in its complete equipoise or absence of difference "includes itself and the presence of difference" (Ib.), that it is not only "A" but includes both "A" and a not-A

or "B" (Ib. 8, 213-4; 7, 426; 9, 235), this re-formulation of the
original principle gives it a close affinity to the interweaving of
the composite and differentiated unities in sections C.

The distinction between this absolute Subject and God is
"very important"! "If one of the most eminent mystics of an
earlier time has ventured to speak of a Superdivinity we shall be
permitted to do the same, emphasizing thereby that the Absolute—that absolute Subject—is not to be interchanged directly
with God." "He who shall place himself at the starting point
of the truly free philosophy must therefore give up God himself; whosoever would find it shall lose it and whosoever would
lose it shall find it. He who has once forsaken all and has himself
been forsaken of all and who has seen himself alone with the
infinite, he also has come to the foundation of himself and has
known the whole depth of life—a great step which Plato compares
with death." "Whoever will truly philosophize must be free
from all hope, all desire, all longing, he must desire nothing, know
nothing, feel himself poor and naked, give up everything in order
to win everything" (W. I, 9, 217-8).

This seems to be the same as saying that the eternal Freedom
(the absolute Subject, the Superdivinity) is the pure consciousness which is the same as unconsciousness, and may be linked with
other passages. "We cannot think an eternal consciousness;
such a consciousness would be equal to consciouslessness."
"Pure knowing is not yet that which knows" and "all consciousness has consciouslessness as its foundation." "We are not, of
course, to think that God has been for a time unconscious and
then has become conscious; what *is* thinkable is that in the same
indivisible act of becoming conscious both the consciousless and
the conscious was apprehended by God, the conscious as the
eternal present but the consciousless with the determining of the
eternal past" (W. I, 8, 262). "The great moment, the hour
of philosophy's true birth," and, we may add analogically, the
hour of the birth of a conscious God, is when "thinking resists
knowing itself and now sees itself over against the absolute
Subject" (Ib. 9, 237).

B. "The life of God bears the closest analogy to the life of
man." "All living existence begins from consciouslessness."

"The whole of life is essentially only a continual heightening of consciousness." "Consciousness begins from that instant in which we become aware of the two principles in us, when we subdivide ourselves, when we set ourselves against ourselves, when with the better part of us we raise ourselves above the lower." "The same holds true of God" (W. I, 7, 432-3). "Consciousness" in God begins in the process of world creation, before he has become completely conscious. Cosmogony is theogony. We recognized above the distinction between nature as the ground of God and God. Nature, in fact, is the nature of God, God's nature; it is that which is necessary in God, "the necessity of God is what we call the nature of God" (Ib. 210).

(1) The designations of the two principles that constitute "the duality in God" are somewhat changed. Regarding the real principle, in the place of the "ground for existence," the "real in God" is simply "existence" (or the "non-existing"). "The real, consciousless is the existence of God purely as such. The existence of God, however, is not the same as God himself"; it is the predicate of the existing (W. I, 7, 435). Again, it is the "instinctive half-conscious wisdom" which contains the possibility of the intelligence that it has not yet become (Ib. 8, 66); it is "longing" (Ib. 170) and is like the half-conscious condition of dreaming (Ib. 280-1). It is the "irrational principle" that influences the world structure (Ib. 328). We would expect this mere longing to be analogous to the unrestricted expansion as was the "longing" that needed to be disciplined by the "understanding," yet, as the "will of the ground" was opposed to the "universal Will," so we find that this principle, as opposed to the Love that seeks not its own, is egoistic, self-centered, a restricting "no" (Ib. 211); "egoism is the real in God" (Ib. 7, 439).

(2) On the other hand is the ideal principle. "The ideal in God is the existing" (W. I, 7, 430); "the ideal is the existing God or God *sensu eminenti*. For, strictly speaking, we always understand by God the existing God. The ideal or conscious is the subject of existence" (Ib. 435-6). It is the rational or spiritual principle, "as it were the savior and deliverer of nature" (Ib. 8, 248). In opposition to the centripetal force of egoism, it is the

self-giving "yes" (Ib. 214). The "ideal in God," "God himself" or the "true God" is Love (Ib. 7, 439). If these two principles remained in perfect equilibrium neither God nor anything could develop; "the true reality of God consists directly in their activity and reciprocity" (Ib.).

In a brief reference to the final period of Schelling's Philosophy of Nature we mentioned his designation for the three stages of nature: (A^1) Matter, (A^2) Light, (A^3) Life. Now that nature is the nature of God and his whole philosophy has become a doctrine of "God," we find him relating the eternal principles to stages of God's revelation and designating them "potencies" in "God" (W. I, 8, 309), that is, for the word comes from algebra, God's involution, or God raised successively to a higher power.

In the process by which "God" comes to consciousness the differentiated unity offers at first a preponderance of the real. "In the yet unconscious condition God has, it is true, the two principles in himself, but without setting himself up as the one or the other, that is, without taking cognizance of himself in the one or the other. This cognizance appears along with the nascent consciousness, that is, God sets himself up as the first potency, as consciousless, but he cannot, as real, contract himself without, as ideal, expanding himself; he cannot, as real, set himself up as object without, as ideal, setting himself up *at the same time* as subject" (Ib. 7, 434). "Between the two potencies there is a priority and posteriority; the real is *natura prius*, the ideal is *natura posterius*. The lower potency is therefore set up, of course, *before* the higher, not, however, according to dignity but according to existence" (Ib. 427).

C. We now consider the principles as a composite unity whose revelation needs the differentiated unity (W. I, 7, 421) but whose perfect equilibrium still persists—"disregarding their opposition, the two principles are one" (Ib. 445). "The real in God is existence, the ideal is the existing; that in which real and ideal are one is the actually existing living God," "God as A^3" (Ib. 430). This unity in which the ideal is limited by the real is the basis of ascribing personality to God. "All personality rests on a dark ground" (Ib. 413). "There is something in God which is not God himself" (Ib. 458). "So long as the God of modern Theism remains the simple nature that he is in all newer systems, so long as in God there is not recognized an actual duality and over against the affirming, expanding force, a limiting, denying force posited, so long the affirmation of a personal God is that lack of sincerity which the truly candid Kant so much lamented in these matters" (Ib. 8, 73). "All agree that the Godhead is purest love, infinitely expressed. Yet they wish it at the same time to exist as such. Existence is particularization. The love that seeks not its own cannot therefore of itself be existing. The essence of all essences is the opposite of personality, therefore another force must produce a basis for it. A force of egoity is required that the love exist in a particularized way and for itself" (Ib. 210 abrv.)

To this unity which is the "copula" of the opposites, the unity of the "ground" and the "grounded," of "no" and "yes" (W. I, 8, 214; 301), treated now as a third potency, as "A^3," of which the other two potencies are a condition and to which they have led (Ib. 242), he applies the designation "World-Soul." This, we recall, was his designation for nature's primal force in his second period as we have arranged them. "If now that first potency, in virtue of which the necessary essence shut itself up in itself, is looked upon as the first ground of nature, and the second potency is looked upon as the intellectual world standing over against it, we cannot be in doubt as to the meaning of the third. It is the universal soul by means of which the universe is inspired, and which, in its immediate relation to the Godhead, is master of it and is in full possession of its own mental faculties; it is the eternal bond between nature and the mental world and between the world and God, the immediate instrument with which God alone works in nature and the mental world" (Ib. 252).

This composite unity continues in the process the perfect equilibrium, so to speak, of the opposites as they were as a pure original unity; or, in Schelling's words: "Nature set up at the beginning, although at the very beginning only a potency of the divine life, is still whole in itself and equal to the whole (the eternal nature). It is not a part of the divine substance, but the whole Godhead dwells in it, in so far as it apprehends itself, encloses and delimits itself in itself. At the very beginning the divine unity lay as the basis of the opposition (A & B) that is in it, though hidden and quiescent. The denying force in it is that which precedes and is related as first potency; the essence (A) set up by it inwardly is that which follows, and is thus related as a second potency. The most inward of all in it, however, the essential essence, was neither the one nor the other, but the secret bond, the hidden force of oneness, that which is A³ in it itself" (W. I, 8, 276).

By the application of the theory of potencies to "nature in God" at the same time as this has become "the nature *of* God," there has appeared a triad of potencies in God which is to form the basis of Schelling's final Theology. And "God" is more than his three potencies. The "nature of God" is, as we noticed, but "the necessity of God." Above the necessity of his nature God abides in his freedom. "Nature is not God for it belongs to that aspect of God which he is necessarily"; "taken strictly, God is called God only according to his freedom" (W. I, 8, 244).

To classify this "God" we can only identify him with the pure original unity (sections A) which, again, was not strictly to be called God! This initial unity is "that eternal Freedom, which is above all nature and out of which everything comes" (W. I, 9, 242). It is pure Freedom or pure contentless Will which somehow includes difference, that is, Will which is also *willing* or eternal world-creation with its constant interplay and equilibrium of forces. "Only God can break the absolute identity of his essence" (Ib. 7, 429), and: "That decision of God to reveal himself came out of his purest freedom" (Ib. 8, 307). Though the problem of Man's "fall" from the Absolute has received consideration, when "God" and his "potencies" (considered not as successive stages but as simultaneous powers or possibilities yonside of time) quietly displace "unconscious Productivity" as the world-creative force, that "break" or "decision" will provide the problem in its final form.

With regard to the "continual strife between the ruling Theism and Naturalism or Pantheism," any scientific grounding of Theism is impossible if the absolute opposition between

VII

The Triune God

(*Munich, 1827-1841; Berlin, 1841-1854*)

The last twenty-seven years of Schelling's life are divided between Munich and Berlin. At the call of King Ludwig Schelling returned from Erlangen to Munich in 1827 and became Professor in the newly founded University and Director of the Academy of Fine Arts. Through the influence of Cousin, the contemporary French authority on German Philosophy, he was elected to the Legion of Honor and the Paris Academy. For five years he was tutor to the crown prince who studied his philosophy enthusiastically and later, as Maximilian II, awarded him the Grand Cross of the Bavarian Order of Merit and a place among the first Knights of his Order founded for the recognition of Art and Science (Kuno Fischer, pp. 190-222; 272-276).

As Professor at Munich his lectures on the "History of Modern Philosophy" review the historical development of systems and point to the change in the conception of philosophy itself that is provided by him now that he has supplemented his earlier "negative" philosophy by a "positive" philosophy, and those on "Philosophical Empiricism" present the "potencies in God" as the positive conditions for explaining nature and history.

For the rest he taught his Philosophy of Mythology and of Revelation of which the Introduction to the latter is also entitled "The Grounding of the Positive Philosophy." As far back as 1793 he had published a study of "Myths, Legends and Philosophical Ideas of the Primitive World." The old love has survived but the motive is new. The massive and ingenious work that fills two thousand pages of his complete works, which, in the "happy combination and fineness of feeling with which he has grouped and mastered the bulky material of the history of religions, is thoroughly akin and equal in rank to the Hegelian treatment" (Windelband), offers an account of the theogonic process in human consciousness as the topstone of a philosophy interested finally in a positive knowledge of God.

Of his lectures Schelling had many hearers, but hearers only. Finally the reading public became acquainted with his new standpoint and his opposition to Hegelianism when, in 1833, he published a preface to Becker's German translation of Cousin's preface to his "*Fragments philosophiques.*" The roots of his new standpoint could be traced back to his Würzburg period when still in his twenties; in fact, as we shall see, the problem to which it addresses itself goes back to his minority.

Schelling's estrangement from Hegel dated from the latter's publication of the "The Phenomenology of Mind" in 1807. After reading the preface of this work Schelling could not make out with precision what the difference of opinion between them was, nor had Hegel made it clear that his polemic applied to false reports about him rather than to himself (L. II, 124). Now that Hegel had completed his work Schelling looked back upon his former friend's philosophy as a "dismal episode." Because Hegel had not advanced beyond the standpoint of Schelling's System of Identity of 1801, his philosophy stands outside of the true course of philosophical development (L. III, 63; 67).

To understand Schelling's criticism it is necessary to distinguish, in everything that is actual, "two wholly different things to know *what* an existing is, *quid sit*, and to know *that* it is, *quod sit*. The former, the answer to the question as to *what* it is, provides me insight into the *nature* of the thing, or it enables me to understand the thing, to have a conception of it, or to have the *thing itself* in the conception. The latter, however, the insight *that* it is does not provide me with the mere conception but with something extending beyond the mere conception, which is the existence" (W. II, 3, 57-8). In other words, we are to distinguish the *negative* conditions, or those without which something cannot be, from the *positive* conditions, or those through which something exists in actuality (cf. above p. 18–9).

With this distinction in mind, Schelling looks upon his System of Identity as a merely negative philosophy. Its basis was the oneness of creative reason in the universe with the thinking reason in the human mind, the unity of the objective and the subjective reason, the identity of existence and thought. This philosophy can determine only that which is "not *not* to be thought" (W. I, 10, 211). While prescribing the conditions under which anything that exists must be thought, it does not determine actual existence. In a word, Reason cannot stand alone as the principle of philosophy. The value of Rationalism is negative and needs to be supplemented by a positive philosophy: "that anything actually exists, even that which comes from reason, only experience can teach" (W. II, 3, 58), "that *that* which is constructed actually exists only experience tells, not the reason." Experience is the control that assures rational knowledge that its *a priori* invention is not a chimera (Ib. 62).

Hegel's philosophy is a negative philosophy and a bad one. In equating conception with actuality he has renewed the fundamental error of ontology, setting up for his time a "new Wolfianism"; or he goes back to the standpoint of Scholasticism, beginning with a purely rational conception excluding everything empirical (W. I, 10, 212-3). This episode "has at least served to show that it is impossible with the pure reason to reach actuality" (Ib.).

Kant's criticism of the Ontological Argument has clearly shown that it is impossible to cull existence out of the conception. Of course, whatever exists must exist in the manner in which thought looks upon it as necessary. "There is a logical necessity in things" (W. II, 3, 61), but the logical is merely the "negative of existence" and "it far from follows that everything exists only *by means of* the logical" as, e. g., everything in the sensible world is conceived in number and mass, but that does not mean that geometry or arithmetic explain the sensible world; in the world there is obviously something other and more than mere reason (W. I, 10, 143-4).

Instead of Schelling's own principle of necessary progress, which is "the *only* real discovery in post-Kantian philosophy" (W. II, 1, 334), namely, the living and active subject-object or absolute Subject that according to its nature objectifies itself and returns to itself in evolutionary stages, Hegel has set up "the logical conception to which through the most curious fiction or hypostatization he ascribes a similarly necessary self-movement" (W. I, 10, 212). The Hegelian philosophy speaks only of the conceptions of things and of relations that the objects assume in mere thinking and its fundamental failure is seen when it tries to make itself into a positive philosophy (W. II, 3, 80); the goal it aims at it cannot reach, it cannot bridge "the ugly broad ditch" that separates logic from nature. There comes a point beyond which the dialectic movement cannot go. On the brink of actuality it suffers shipwreck: "the Idea unlocks Nature," or "releases itself out of itself as Nature or in the form of being otherwise" (W. I, 10, 153), or "Nature is the falling away from the Idea" (W. II, 3, 89). Such phrases signal Hegel's distress and in them an act of Will is implied.

Soon after Hegel's death in 1831 Schelling's call to Berlin was discussed in influential quarters but he was not appointed to succeed him. He was finally invited in 1840 to take a "position as unique as the personality" to whom the position was offered, to come not as an ordinary professor but as one chosen by God to be the teacher of the hour, whose proximity the king desired for his own strengthening, and, though free to please himself in the matter of lecturing, to correct the "fanaticism of the (Hegelian) school of empty concepts." In Munich Roman Catholic influences were in the ascendant and the Faculty of Philosophy had come under pedagogical restrictions repulsive to Schelling (Fischer, pp. 236; 239; 232). In accepting the call to Berlin he saw before him the opportunity of solving the burning questions of the time. During the decade before his coming critical investigations into the psychological and documentary origins of religious faith were agitating the public mind and the works of Bauer, Vatke, Straus and Feuerbach were being widely read.

In his opening address (1841) Schelling meets the extraordinary tension which his appearance excited by an equally extraordinary conception of its importance. "I feel the full significance of this moment." "Were I not of the conviction that I can through my presence perform a service for philosophy greater than I have ever earlier been in a position to perform I would not be standing here before you." Forty years earlier he had opened a new page in the history of philosophy; one side had been filled, circumstances have now called him to the metropolis of German

Philosophy to turn over the page and fill the other side with a philosophy granting longingly desired disclosures and broadening the consciousness of men beyond its previous limits (W. II, 4, 359-360). He came as an ambassador of peace to reconcile a world rent by so many factions (Ib. 366; L. III, 168).

For five years he lectured in the University upon the Philosophy of Revelation and Mythology. The influence of this philosophy was negligible. His lectures were the same as they had been ten years earlier (W. II, 4, 231). Upon the recent investigations of Biblical criticism he looked down from the height of what seemed to the world an abstruse scholasticism. All he published was a preface to the posthumous works of Steffens. In this he writes for the times demanding an end of the church Confession, which merely seeks "agreement with Holy Scripture without proving the real truth of the matter" (W. I, 10, 403), a new Theology, which is neither formal as the scholastic, nor pectoral as the pious, nor blind as the orthodox, not superficial as the rationalistic, but which is breathed through by the free air of science, and freedom for philosophy, which is not to be forbidden contact with positive religion.

His first lectures in Berlin were reported and offered to the public *verbatim* by Paulus, with prolix comment to show the "emptiness" of his philosophy. Others looked upon him as "the modern παιδαγωγός εἰς Χριστον," "the *spiritus rector* of the century." When, in 1846, the appeal of Paulus against the legal ban that had been placed upon his "pirated" work was successful, Schelling ceased to lecture (Fischer, pp. 262-8). Later addresses in the Academy extended to 1852 and form parts of his final work, the "Philosophical Introduction to the Philosophy of Mythology, or, An Account of the Purely Rational Philosophy" (W. II, 1, vi).

The foregoing indicates the comprehensiveness of Schelling's final philosophical outlook and is in keeping with his life-long zest for final principles. He has not renounced his negative philosophy for a positive (W. II, 3, 132: "No one can treasure the rational philosophy more highly than I"); he offers a combination of the rational principles that determine the manner in which what exists must exist (the "what" of things) with the positive principle that determines actual existence (the "that" of things). "The 'positive philosophy' belongs not only to the most uninvestigated parts of philosophical literature but also to the most rich in problems" (Tillich) while the "rational philosophy treats of the most difficult problems that are given to the mind of man" (Groos).

In a Theory of Knowledge that now combines the *a posteriori* "that" with the *a priori* "what" we can anticipate the result for our subject. God, as the absolute "That," will be a necessary presupposition, but, as absolute, baffling any attempt at conceptual formulation, while God, considered in relation to the "What" of things, whose totality he also is, will acquire a conceptual content that can be theologically systematized.

The divisions of the remainder of this chapter present the same themes as the similarly lettered divisions of our last chapter and thus comparison is facilitated and specific reference to similarities and differences rendered superfluous.

A. We may take Descartes' Ontological Argument as an illustration of the inadequacy of Rationalism. According to Descartes God is necessarily existent; that is, it is impossible for him not to exist. There is thus excluded from God the possibility of not existing. Since, however, if anything is possible only so long as its opposite is also possible, when you exclude from God the possibility of not existing you exclude from him the possibility of existing. Moreover, if God were simply the necessarily existent without any possibility, a plus would have to be added to make him "God," and this Descartes' ontology cannot supply (W. I, 10, 14-22). Similarly all systems of modern philosophy serve to show that the purely rational *a priori* judgment gives content only and is negative in relation to existence. Absolute Idealism, their final completion, is not, as such, concerned with the question of existence (Ib. 149).

If philosophy is to explain the actual world and its course of events as well as the logical world, positivism must share the throne with a-priorism. There is a "That" that anticipates not only all thinking but every existence that appears in thinking, a "That" that is existentially prior to the common product of existence and thought. It is thus an "un- and pre-thought (unvordenkliche) existence" (W. II, 3, 268). This "absolute Prius" must be the absolutely prius for if it were not, something before it would be, and this would be the "absolute Prius" (Ib. 161). "The ultimate question is ever, Why is there something, why is there not nothing?" This cannot be shown through thinking, but the Idealist's doubt as to whether there is a something truly existing presupposes a truly existing (Ib. 242), something that precedes everything that goes forth out of potency. "The absolute beginning certain through itself" cannot be proved, nor can necessary motion be ascribed to the conception of it (Ib. 129). This pure original "That" comes forth in no conception (Ib. 164). It may be designated "pure actuality itself" (W. II, 1, 391), or "the self-Existing, αὐτο τo ὄν" (Ib. 314). To this absolute Individual, considered apart from or unrelated to any "What," the term " God" is inappropriately applied. This absolutely unrelated can only be called the "*prius* of the Godhead" (Ib. 3, 160; cf. ib. 1, 588).

(A) The business of the rational or negative philosophy is to "unveil the inner organism of reason" (W. II, 3, 76). It deals with the rational demonstration of the principles grounded in pure reason. It analyzes the conception of the "Existing" (which is distinguished from the "self-Existing") in relation to thinking. In what manner can the Existing not *not* be thought? It turns out that Kant's "conception of an object in general" (Cf. W. I, 10, 233), if it is not to be the conception of a merely possible existence that cannot be known, must be the conception of that which can become known. "The reason is, according to Kant, nothing other than the general capacity for knowledge," and by considering this "capacity" reason becomes the "infinite potency of knowledge" (W. II, 3, 62. As the word "possibility" is used in discussions of the presuppositions of experience, so Schelling now uses the word "potency" in discussing the presuppositions of "existence as a whole in all its gradations"; it also connotes inherent *potentia* or "might" as "potentiality" when formally distinguished from "actuality" may not).

As certainly as reason is, which can be questioned only in its name, and as its immediate content is the conception of an existence in general, so all must agree that this is "infinite potency" (Ib. 74). "Since to all knowledge an existence corresponds, to actual knowledge an actual existence, the infinite potency of knowledge cannot be other than the infinite potency of existence" (Ib. 64). If Schelling has said earlier that you must give up not only "father and child" but "God himself" in order to philosophize, we see now that he is speaking against "the well-known theologians and philosophers who make God the immediate content of reason; this is contradicted here, for by God we must still think of something actual" (Ib. 74-5). "The beginning of philosophy is that which is before the actual existence" (Ib. 204); "we have found the place where man makes himself free not merely from revelation but from *everything* actual, where is as yet met only the infinite potency of all existence" (Ib. 76 abrv.). It is in this infinite potency that there is discovered immediately an inner and necessary organism of successive potencies (Ib.).

(B, 1) The first potency ("—A") of the Existing in general is "ability to exist." This ability is to be thought of necessarily as the non-existent (Aristotle's μὴ ὄν, the relatively non-existent; not οὐκ ὄν, the absolutely non-existent. W. II, 1, 288). Thus the "ability to be," in spite of its negative character, is not nothing; it is the first step in the analysis of the conception of existence. The non-existent, or, if you will, Kant's "totality of all possibility" (Cf. ib. 287), *is*, and must be thought of not as mere hypothesis but as "ability to exist"; this is an "inevitable conception" (Ib. 2, 39). Moreover nothing is definable except in terms of Will—"object" (Gegenstand) means "re-ject" (Widerstand. Ib. 3, 206), and, specifically, "ability to be" is quiescent will (Ib. 2, 36).

(B, 2) The second potency (" + A") of the Existing is "the pure existing." Reason is dissatisfied with the element of contingency in "ability to exist" (W. II, 3, 66) and "ability to exist," taken by itself, cannot be a full account of existence. Reason must conceive this "pure existing" to keep a place for the "ability to exist" to occupy without thereby ceasing to be "ability to exist." The "pure existing" is a sort of compensation for the existence that the "ability to exist" does not become. This "pure existing" also is a μὴ ὄν, it is a non-existence in a still higher degree than is the "ability to exist." In contrast to the "ability to exist," which, as quiescent will, has an innateness to become "willing," the "pure existing" is desireless or unselfish will. Existence as "the pure existing" is *pure* will and cannot of itself go over into *willing*, it can only do so through mediation, and for this it requires that aspect of itself in which it is "ability to exist" (Ib. 210-215).

(C) The third and last determination or potency ("$\pm$ A") of the Existing is the unity of the "ability to exist" and the "pure existing." It is not a union of parts or elements but a substantial identity, the whole Existing is "ability to exist" and the same whole Existing is the "pure existing." Thought was compelled to proceed to this moment in the analysis of the conception of the Existing; dissatisfied with the two separated *momenta*, the "ability to exist" and the "pure existing," it must have the conception of an existence in general, the conception of a potency of all existence, which, as potency, precedes all actual existence, and, without losing this *a priori* potential character, is also pure freedom to be or not to be.

Expressed in terms of will, an identity of quiescent will and pure will is required; in terms of the subject-object relation, "we want the subject which, as such, and without ceasing to be a subject, that is, to be pure might, is an object, and we want the object which, in that it is an object—existing—does not cease to be a subject, a *potentia pura existendi*" (W. II, 2, 55-6). And what "we want" is found: "If we define the ability to exist as a subject, and define the pure existing as an object, then the third is that which is neither merely the second nor merely the first, but which is the inseparable subject-object which, if it goes over into existence as an object, does not cease to be a subject, and does not, in order to be a subject, give up an object, i. e., existing, —that which is able not to lose itself, that which remains with itself, in short, that which is able to exist existing as such" (Ib. 3, 235). For this third determination of the Existing "language has no other name than Mind." (Ib. 2, 57).

We are now in a position to obtain a rational conception of God as the first principle of philosophy. The absolute "That," the "self-Existing," considered apart from any relation, could

only be called the "*prius* of the Godhead," not "God." Newton
has said, audaciously but truly, "*Deus est vox relativa*" (W. I,
10, 261). The "self-Existing" must now be viewed together with
the "Existing" which is a totality of the three potencies (W. II,
3, 78). Schelling's result of this union of the "That" and the
"What" we may express simply as: *Deus = existentia essentiae +
essentia existentiae.*

God is the union of the self-existing and the existing. On the
one hand, if God were thought of as only the existing he would
then not exist for the existing is only an analysis of the conception
of existence and does not give actual existence. The existing,
"the idea of total possibility," taken alone has no existence. Unlike the self-existing, which is free from all generality and potentiality, the existing is a universal, and "universals do not exist"
(W. II, 1, 586). But when the self-existing and the existing are
put together, the existing gets existence—the potencies of the existing become attributes of the self-existing. "Not the subject, not
the object, not the subject-object *Is*, but the determined One
is the subject, is the object, is the subject-object, that is, these
elements which might appear as principles are reduced to mere
attributes of the One" (Ib. 317).

On the other hand, if God were only the self-existing, only
pure "That," the term "God" could mean nothing, he could not
be thought; there could be no conception of him for this is provided only by the existing, by the "what" of things, by the Idea
of total possibility. Therefore we may again put together the
self-existing and the existing and now as God's existence plus
God's thinking. "God contains in himself nothing except the
pure That of his own existence; but that he *is* would not be true
if he were not *something*—something of course not in the sense
of an existing but in the sense of all existing,—if he had not a
relation to thinking, a relation not to a *conception* but to *the
conception of all conceptions*, to the *Idea*. Here is the true place
for that unity of existence and thinking" (Ib. 587). Although
"existence" and "thinking" are thus united in God, they are,
however, only truly placed if "existence" comes first. "In this
unity the priority is not on the side of thinking." "The way goes

not from the universal to the individual." "The existing is the
first, the thinking only the second or subsequent" (Ib.).

In the foregoing briefly summarized adventure into the inner
organism of mind we have reached Schelling's final analysis of
the first principle of philosophy. It is not only the pure original
unity of an abstract identity, but is this unity plus the composite unity that is now a triad of potencies initially at rest or in
equilibrium. It is the principle according to which all existence
must be thought. It lies at the basis of all existence, and the
search for it was compelled by the inborn impulse for the One in
All, which, being unconditioned, is the basis of all deduction and
the object of unconditioned knowledge (W. II, 1, 296).

The name given earlier to the equipment necessary for this
adventure was "intellectual perception"; it was not "faith" or
"feeling." In this period, as we shall see later (§D) "immediate
knowledge" belongs to the Ur-man; to the philosopher it is
now "an experience in pure thinking." "That nothing precedes
the pure Subject, you must experience. Experience, I say. There
are many quite intelligent men who are prejudiced against the
exclusive power of pure thinking in philosophy because they
begin with the limited view of induction which has hitherto been
the only one taught in the schools." "There are two kinds of
experience. The one says what actually is and is not, which is
the common use of the word; the other says what is possible and
impossible, this is acquired in thinking. As we sought the
elements of the Existing we were determined by what is possible
and impossible in thinking. What the *momenta* of the Existing
were and how we arranged them was not in our choice, but, in
thinking of what the Existing is, of what can be thought as the
Existing, and especially of what is the *primum cogitabile*, they
were there *to be actually investigated*, therefore *to be experienced*"
(Ib. 326).

What is acquired in thinking in this way admits, of course, of
no proof except *ad hominem* but the philosopher's inner dialogue
(Cf. W. I, 10, 98) satisfies him, he has "remembered" trans-
cendentally the nature of reality (Ib. 95). And the self-Existing
"is the existence in which thinking has its *goal:* if we come by it,
thinking is completed and finds its complete satisfaction; what

is possible in virtue of thinking, what is permitted to think itself, *has been thought*, therefore is there nothing more to be thought *beyond* this existence, therefore also it is no longer to be doubted, it is the absolutely undoubted existence" (W. II, 1, 320).

B. The first task of the *positive* philosophy is to explain the creation or the *actuality* of the world-process. The question of its *possibility* belongs to the purely rational or *negative* philosophy: "How is it possible that —A, +A, ±A can be a consequence of A°?" (W. II, 1, 570). Since in the potencies are contained the forms outside of which nothing can exist, since they are the principles or the true initial conceptions of all existence, the coming into existence of the world is to be explained in terms of the potencies. The equilibrium of the potencies is disturbed, they are "set in tension." The complexity of the situation after that takes place need not be fully recounted here; sufficient to say that the possibility for the "setting in tension" is found in the first potency, in that aspect of the "Existing" in which it is "ability to be." The creation of the world out of nothing is not a creation out of absolutely nothing (οὐκ ὄν) but out of a not-existing (μὴ ὄν) that is "ability to exist" (W. I, 10, 282-5), and thus its possibility is explained. The three potencies are "cosmic, demiurgic causes" and in the process that is at once cosmogonic and theogonic the first potency is the "substrate of the whole" (W. II, 3, 290). The problem of the beginning of time in eternity is dealt with similarly, the middle member between eternity and time is the first potency of the will, the "divine imagination" (Ib. 293; 307-9).

The "Existing," whose condition is now "reversed" by the reciprocal tension of its three potencies, is the One (*unum*) turned (*versum*); the process is the Universe (W. II, 2, 90; I, 10, 311). Thus the universe is not God as the "self-Existing" but God "turned about" in the process of the "Existing." Creation both reveals God and veils him. The world is God's Irony. God dissembles; "the existence of a world distinguished from God (for the potencies in their tension are no longer God) rests on the divine skill in dissimulation which affirms as an appearance what it is his intention to deny"; "for the most part he sets forth the opposite of what he really wills." "No one has thought of applying this (conception of irony) to the explanation of the world itself" and to the way in which God works (W. II, 2, 91-2).

The *a priori* rational philosophy is confined within that sphere of "possibility." To account for the *actuality* of the world-process, for that which is "*a priori* inconceivable" (W. II, 3, 165), is the first task of the positive philosophy. This is the problem that has haunted each chapter. In 1795 it was the chief business of Philosophy to solve the problem of passing from the infinite to the finite, of the origin of a sphere of experience, of the Absolute going out of itself (above p. 13); the only thinkable creation out of nothing was the world that steps forth with the free selfconscious creature (p. 18; cf. p. 23.) In 1800 limitedness in general was theoretically explicable, but that the same act should provide a particular limitedness falling within a definite point of time was the inconceivable and inexplicable of all philosophy and led from the theoretical to the pragmatic in the "System of Transcendental Idealism" (p. 31). In 1802 the existence of the finite in time is attributed to an action of its own will before all time (p. 42). In 1804 the possibility of the falling away of the Idea or the Eternal World was explained, but its actuality was inexplicable (p. 54). In 1809 the egoity of the prototypical man's act of absolute freedom was attributed to the will of the existence in God but not God (p. 63), and if the question of the coming into existence of this not-God out of the absolute identity faces our philosopher again, in 1811 he can only say that God alone can break his absolute identity or that the decision of God to reveal himself came out of the purest freedom (p. 70).

Refusing a philosophical construction of existence which, to use a mathematical simile, is not simply a curve graphed in asymptotic relation to its axes, he must determine the point at which the curve leaves the horizontal axis. His "positive" philosophy in its entirety can be taken as an answer to that problem; specifically, the absolute "That" in relation to the "What" of things is their "Lord." At the point where the curve of finite existence begins its upward movement stands God; he stands outside of the sphere of reason's necessity in absolute freedom to start or not to start the world-process.

In this last period wherever Schelling faces the problem its

solution is difficult until his final declaration. That "first beginning" in which that which is "as nothing" turns about and
becomes "something" is an "initial contingent" (W. I, 10, 101).
If it is "scarcely possible to make clear" in what way God sets
up existence, the difficulty is taken away by regarding it as
willed by his "immanent will, a will that moves itself alone"
(Ib. 277). Although all beginning lies in the "ability to exist"
the ability to be the "ability to exist" or the capacity of original
initiative cannot be denied to God for to be without this ability
would be "the greatest weakness" (Ib. 279). Although God,
who, having the potencies or principles of existence within
him must begin something, is under a certain measure of necessity, yet he is "absolutely free" when he sets up the potencies *as
potencies:* "they would not be potencies (i. e., possibilities of
a future existence) without his will" (Ib. 282). An analysis of the
conception of the divine existence gives us a God who *is* not, but
who, *if* he were, as well as being according to the forms provided
by the three potencies, must be "pure freedom to be and not to
be" (W. II, 2, 58).

Again, the oft-repeated misunderstanding of the rational
philosophy makes God only God through the world, and only
absolute mind through the finite mind. The rational philosophy
so understood cannot get beyond a mere logical movement. Of
course God is God only in relation to the world; "God is only
God as the Lord, but he is not Lord without something over
which he is Lord. But God is Lord of the world already *before*
the world, namely, to set it up or not to set it up" (W. II, 3, 291).
As Kant's Criticism led to the humiliation of the reason so the
negative philosophy comes to its judgment and crisis when the
"Idea" which was the goal, God as the one found last, is thrust
out of the "Idea." "The truly Existing is that which is outside
of the Idea, is not the Idea, but is more than the Idea, κρεῖττον
τοῦ λόγου" (Ib. 1, 566). The positive philosophy takes that
which exists necessarily in the conception and brings it to the
place "where it proves itself as an actual (existing) Lord of existence (of the world), as a personal, actual God, by which at the
same time every other existence, as derived from that first That,

has its existence explained, and thus there is established a positive system, that is, one that explains actuality" (Ib. 564).

Actuality is thus finally explained in "the absolute Mind" which is not "the mind that is not able not to be mind" (the third potency) but which is "*free* Mind," free from all compulsion, "that transcendent, superabounding Freedom, the thought of which so expands all our vessels of thought and knowledge that we feel we have now reached the highest, than which a higher cannot be thought. Freedom is our highest, our Godhead; this we want as the final cause of things" (W. II, 3, 256). This positive philosophy is the free philosophy, you may take it or leave it, but if you stand by the rational philosophy alone you cannot have "the actual God, the actual course of events, nor a free relation of God to the world" (Ib. 132).

C. With the beginning of the process actualized, although the potencies are set in reciprocal tension their unity is not thereby destroyed. This unifying function in the *becoming* belongs to the World-Soul, not now the unity of the first and second potencies and termed "A^3," which unity, as "$\pm A$," has become only the third potency, but, in a context in which the three potencies are termed "causes," "the fourth cause." The World-Soul, which was the "absolute-One" of his second period and closely akin to the "unconscious Productivity" of his third, is now, in the terms of the rational philosophy, to be distinguished from both the "self-Existing" and the "Existing." The "self-Existing" acted as a unifying bond of the three potencies of the "Existing" *before* they were set in tension; similarly the World-Soul acts as a unifying bond of the three potencies of the "Existing" *after* they are set in tension. It works in all things especially the organic. For this conception the word "mind" (or "spirit") is inappropriate for "mind" is able to rend itself free from the material, but "soul" must have something of which it is the soul. If by means of the tension of the potencies the "Existing" becomes matter, through matter goes the immaterial World-Soul, which, similar to the "self-Existing" in being above the "Existing," is different from it in not being able to exist absolutely for itself. This World-Soul is not a part of existence but equals the whole. As the soul of all things it is their *being* only in so far as all things express in themselves the whole. The rational philosophy must use this conception to enable it to give an account of becoming (W. II, 1, 399-415; cf. I, 10, 110-117).

Schelling is convinced that his philosophy has done a unique service to Theology. His Philosophy of Nature had turned all the best thinkers from an "unnatural supernaturalism" and made for ever an end of that "weak Theism" whose God is not simply "above" the world but also "outside" of it. Unfortunately, in Hegel it had taken a departure into a "clumsy Pantheism" (W. II, 3, 397-8). A purely rational God cannot be personal, "for we only call anything personal when it is free from the universal and *for itself*" (Ib. 1, 281); in the realm of pure reason all personalities would be superfluous (Ib. 539). In distinction from "Theism" and from "Pantheism" he terms his theory "Monotheism," but, since God is the All (the Existing) as well as the Only (the self-Existing), and since this Only is Freedom, the term "Panmonothelism" would be better, to which we would have to add the adjective "personal" to make the title embrace his whole position.

"Deism or Theism," as represented by the writers of the Enlightenment and of the early eighteenth century English Naturalism, could use the word "God" in but a vague or general way, saying "God" but not "*the* God" (W. II, 2, 70). It may attribute personality to God but is incapable of giving definiteness to this idea. If it affirms a selfconsciousness in God this remains meaningless, for selfconsciousness is unthinkable unless it contains at least three: the one conscious, him of whom he is conscious, and the other excluded (Ib. 73-4).

Mere Theism, rejecting the All, the affix $\pi\hat{a}\nu$, is "shallow, absolutely impotent, thoroughly incapable of explaining anything" and its emptiness is the only content of the "so-called purely moralistic and puffed up theory of religion" (Ib. 41). It may affirm a free creation but it robs God of the power of immediate existence, of going out of himself, of becoming unlike himself, of producing anything (Ib.); lacking the "potency of all existence, according to which every existence is only the existence of God" it is unbearable to the religious consciousness (Ib. 69). It may affirm that there is only one God, meaning that "outside of God there is no other God," but such a God is a mere negative totality (Ib. 22); blind to the fact that "the modalities of the divine existence must be the modalities of all existence" (Ib. 60) instead of simply denying the existence of another God it denies every other existence. "If Theology knows no other place for its theory of an only God than under the so-called negative attributes it lacks the essential notion of Monotheism" (Ib. 61-2).

Pantheism, as represented by Spinoza, in including the πᾶν without which Theism was unsatisfactory to both the intellect and the emotions, exercises a charm over all minds. Pantheism is "the ground of the Godhead and of all true religion" (W. II, 2, 68). The thought that "God is the immediate potency of all existence" (Ib.), that "all existence is only the existence of God" is one to which all hearts beat (Ib. 68; 40). Again, it is superior to Theism in recognizing distinctions in God, as those of "extension and thinking." But though "Monotheism and Pantheism lie nearer each other than either lies to Theism" (Ib. 70), Pantheism is inferior to Monotheism. It fails to account for the genetic priority and difference of dignity between the two attributes (W. I, 10, 39-40). Morever, if "blind, lifeless Substance" were the only existence nothing could come out of it nor a living process be accounted for (W. II, 2, 74), and, even when equated with the first potency in God, namely, the "ability to be," it requires the other potencies to make up the "Existing" (W. II, 3, 208f.). It is therefore necessary for Pantheism to be overcome by a true Monotheism within which Pantheism is latent.

"Monotheism" adds the μόνος, the self-Existing, which in relation to the potencies, remains the One and Only above and within them. The "absolute" or "perfect Mind" is both the One and the All. It is the "All": in it alone is existence, its categories are the categories of all existence; the whole mind is in each of its three forms. It is also the "Only" for it is "the indissoluble (spiritual, personal) unity and linkage of the forms" or the "All-ness" of the "All" (W. II, 3, 260; 2, 60-61). In other words, this absolute Mind is the Lord whose oneness consists in his lordship over what without that lordship would be a plurality:

"Hear, O Israel, the Lord thy Elohim is one Lord" (Ib. 2, 47).

In 1802 Schelling symbolized the three unities, or the three aspects of his Absolute, theologically as Father, eternal Son and incarnate Son (above p. 41). Not content with having done Theology the signal service of making Theism = Deism + Pantheism (as these terms are used today), the three potencies derived as necessary phases of the philosopher's experience in pure thinking now tell why religions have had their triad of gods and why "Monotheism" finally developed, in Christian Theology, into Trinitarianism (W. II, 2, 78).

The potencies, in virtue of their relative independence are capable of fellowship and they thus constitute the inner life of God. They form an economical trinity and are, or rather come to be, three personalities. To be "personal" is to be "free from the universal" and "for oneself," to be "outside of reason and according to one's own will" (W. II, 1, 281), and "the God in whose power it stands to set up or not to set up the existence outside of him" is "absolute Personality" which, as the personality that is able to begin everything, "we also call, philosophically, the Father" (Ib. 3, 311).

In reference to the merely natural process prior to the beginning of history, this is the only divine "personality" of which we can speak, but with the appearance of Man (§ D below) the second potency becomes actualized as the "Son," and the third potency —the unity of the other two *as* unity—becomes the "Spirit." Thus "there are three personalities which are as far from being three separate gods as from being merely three different *names* of one and the same personality" (Ib. 335). The subsequent historical process (§ E below) which begins when man rends himself free from God "terminates necessarily in the highest expression of Monotheism, that is, in Christianity" (Ib. 2, 79) and in a theory of the Trinity according to which "God is not merely *in* three personalities, but there are three persons *each* of which is God" (Ib. 4, 65). Schelling's theory of the Trinity is neither the Hegelian nor the ecclesiastical (Ib. 70; 86).

D. As the first task of the Positive Philosophy was to account for the beginning of the natural process by the ascription of absolute freedom to God, we may take, as its second task, the

consideration of the actuality of the beginning of the historical
process initiated by a similar freedom ascribed to the prototypical Man, and with this is joined the task of the Rational
Philosophy to account for its possibility. This Ur-Man sets the
potencies in tension again and in doing so the setting up of the
finite phenomenal world, the world external to the eternal world
of ideas is accomplished (cf. above pp. 53-54).

Around the head of the Ur-Man, of whom all empirical minds
are but effaced images, revolve other questions—the ethical
question as to the responsibility for the world's evil, the philosophical question of individuation or the relation of each
man to the one Man, the anthropological question of the unity
and diversity of the human race—which, though not being
treated by us, indicate his metaphysical and historical importance. He is the microcosm of the macrocosm and as such, after
being symbolized as "A^4," is finally more fittingly symbolized
as "$a°$." "The idealism of Kant and Fichte gains an historical
and ethical character; for the in-itself is here no longer separated
merely logically from the sensible world and set over it, but this
separation is the most characteristic act of the I" (Groos).

When Schelling's Absolute was "unconscious Productivity"
we experienced the utmost difficulty in constructing a finite
product. The product was to represent a perfect equilibrium or
composite unity of the two forces, but, since a perfect equilibrium would mean a cessation of the productivity, the product
had to be also an imperfect equilibrium or a differentiated unity
of the two forces (above pp. 24-25). In other words, unconscious
intellectual perception (or absolute selfconsciousness) can only
become reflective or conscious intellectual perception when its
activity comes to a halt in a finite idea—but then it is no longer
pure original identity (cf. above p. 30). This further recollection
of earlier difficulties helps us again to draw together analogous
problems in this final chapter of exposition.

Man is the goal and crown of nature. The reciprocal tension
of the potencies that marked the natural process now come
to rest in "that which is conscious of itself" and attain a perfect
equilibrium or unity (W. II, 3, 282; I, 10, 272). In this Ur-Man
the World-Soul steps forth in a completed organism as Mind,

a mind which is the counterpart of the divine mind, in immediate relation to it, and able to recognize God for what he is (W. II, 1, 419; 3, 444; 304). The uniqueness of this Mind and its metaphysical significance is seen in its identification with the Aristotelean νοῦς and the Fichtean I. Aristotle's νοῦς—which ought to be taken not as a universal but as an "individual"—was of a wholly different origin from that of the phenomenal forms of the soul, and notwithstanding the dualism that resulted, Aristotle insisted that it stepped into the soul from outside (W. II, 1, 482). The inability to account for the transition from the infinite to the finite is the general failure of Greek Philosophy (Ib. 460f.) It is, however, Fichte's final significance in the history of philosophy that he made the I (which = Aristotle's "active reason") its own act, and termed it a *"Thathandlung"* (an action in the intelligible world; cf. above p. 54). It is thus *causa sui* as is Spinoza's Substance, but in a totally different way (Ib. 420).

We have seen earlier Schelling's "grounding" of this act of freedom which Fichte's Subjective Idealism left "ungrounded" (W. II, 1, 464; cf. 3, 51-57 and above pp. 63, 73). Its possibility is now explained in the God-likeness of the Ur-Man. If it is impossible to pass directly from an infinite Mind with its eternal ideas to a finite world outside of God, it is not unthinkable that this should happen through the mediating World-Soul raised to Mind in the Ur-Man; and if the principle of all existence is God, the principle of all existence external to God can only be that which " = God," namely, the Ur-Mind which is his counterpart. This is, like the Absolute, a "pure That"; it is also "a complete novelty, something which absolutely was not, an entirely new arrival which, since it has no beginning but is its own beginning, *its own act*, is eternal in origin" (W. II, 1, 420-1). It is upon this Will that God "made the fate of his whole work depend" (Ib. 3, 359; cf. 4, 292).

God's eternal world would never have "fallen away" if that "pure act" had not set up a counterpart to him; nor had the sensible world arisen if that mind had remained in its pure perception one with God, if it had not turned its inherent freedom to evil use. But, Prometheus-like, it revealed its fundamental character by acting egoistically; it used its lordship over the potencies to set them in tension again and thus lost its lordship over them, and, as the "Universe" was God's "dissimulation" so the world of finite things is man's "deception"; the phenomenal world which arose, branded by Eden's serpent, disguises the true nature of things (W. II, 1, 486; 464; 2, 151; 3, 366).

This actualization of the finite cannot be accounted for in terms of the Rational Philosophy. Although "you can indeed say that the transition was *natural*, that in virtue of the merely *natural* will as it were it had to take place" (Ib. 3, 360), it turns out that the will finds itself surprised by the result of its act. It believed it could remain in actuality what it was in possibility, but the result presents itself to the will as that which it neither wanted, foresaw nor expected (Ib. 2, 153f.). There is therefore no *a priori* evidence for the Fall, "you can only say that it is, not that it necessarily is; in this sense it is the primary-contingent, the initial-accidental itself," that is, not a contingent that is dependent upon another contingent but that from which every other contingent is derived (Ib. 1, 464).

E. With that "accident" of the Fall we enter the sphere of experience and the realm of history. We may take as the third and final task of the Positive Philosophy the examination of the history of mankind as expressed in all mythologies and religions, and, as such, "the positive philosophy is historical philosophy" (W. II, 1, 571). This is "philosophy" etymologically, and the love of wisdom it displays is a constant and never completed enquiry. As "progressive empiricism" its realm is the religious development of mankind and it shows us "that the *Prius* itself *exists* in the way in which we have *conceived* it, that is, that God exists"; and since this "realm of actuality" is not completed it can offer no final proof but only "a progressive demonstration of the actually existing God, which ever grows and strengthens itself" (Ib. 3, 129-131).

Schelling's presentation of all earth's religions as an organic whole whose elements infer each other and whose development follows phases patterned according to the inner dialectic of pure thinking (God's "potencies") cannot but be of especial interest to students of the Philosophy of Religion. Our own task is completed here in having indicated the answers of the Positive

Philosophy to the major problems of his earlier standpoints. With more consistency, the term "positive" would have been applied only to the final part of this "historical philosophy" or "metaphysical empiricism," namely, the Philosophy of Revelation, the theme of which is Christianity, for while Mythology is presented as a natural and *necessary* development, Revelation rests upon that freedom of God which is above all necessity.

If Schelling has constantly turned from the Absolute as starting-point to the Absolute as goal, a moment's reflection suggests that the problem of ending the process would be no less acute than the problem of beginning it. How can a sphere of finite experience end in an infinite? Reverting to our simile, it is obvious that determining the point at which the curve would meet the vertical axis is but another form of the task of determining the point at which it left the horizontal axis. Though it is not in this other form that the problem has vexed our philosopher, yet with a sure instinct for ultimate problems, redemption also is represented as a non-rational display of the divine freedom. The ideas of revealed religion are not reducible to purely rational truths (W. II, 4, 4); "no *necessity* exists why the human consciousness has held its ground and not been disintegrated in its separation. This can only be the work of a free *Will* which will not permit it to be lost or ruined, and this free Will to uphold and rescue human consciousness can only be sought in that which has willed the world notwithstanding the risk of this ruin" (Ib. 9).

The process through which the human consciousness goes in seeking to regain its lost paradise has two aspects corresponding to the division of philosophy into the Rational and the Positive. It attains a *negative* blessedness through morality, piety, art and the rational philosophy. The essence of the ethical life is the overthrow of that egoity which expressed itself against God in the falling away. Mystical piety prompts a similar self-forgetfulness and the will so abnegates itself that it becomes entirely indifferent even to salvation. Again, true art consists in the completely selfless production that touches the divine blessedness. Finally, "contemplative knowledge" occupies itself with the intelligible world and in pure thinking explores the "what" of things. These, however, do not establish a *positive* blessedness. Kant himself did not perceive the incompleteness of the moral law and had to throw in happiness as something extraneous. The final root of Pietism and its indifference to practical life was the onesidedness of the purely rational philosophy, its mere intellectualism. This can attain to nothing but the God of Aristotle, "the thinking of thinking" (W. II, 1, 555-560).

Truth, beauty, goodness, reason, but not God! The "stages of only a negative blessedness" do not in themselves satisfy the whole of human consciousness, they but make us reach for that which is beyond the "what" of things to that "That" which is the actuality of the "what." If the Rational Philosophy needed a World-Soul to account for "becoming," the Positive Philosophy reflects the passionate demand of the religious consciousness for the Lord of the potencies. "*Him, him* will it have, the God who acts, in whose keeping is a Providence, him who *as a fact himself can oppose the fact of the falling away*, in short, him who is the LORD of existence (not only transmundane but supramundane)" (W. II, 1, 556). "A person seeks a person." "Reason and law do not love, only the personal can love." "The self, as itself a personality, desires personality; it demands a Person who is outside of the world and above the universal and who understands—a Heart that is like its own" (Ib. 566-570).

The goal of history is "the final unity," "the most elevated and most sublime Monotheism which we need to see as the result of all our previous evolution"; and, for those theologians who inveigh against Pantheism to lay to heart, it is the realization of the "Christian or at least Pauline Pantheism" when God will be "all in all" (W. II, 4, 66). As the "Father" was the "absolute Personality" before the process and the "Son" arose during the process, "the future, to which everything is to attain, is the time of the Spirit" (Ib. 71). It is the time of the complete display of an all-embracing Love. Within the history of the Christian religion "Peter is rather the apostle of the Father, Paul is really the apostle of the Son, John is the apostle of the Spirit" (Ib. 326-7). The church's first era was the Petrine; it embraced the Latin peoples and within the Roman church existed as a unity that was grounded on authority and external. It has been followed by the age of Protestant Christianity and

its Germanic adhesion for "in Paul the principle was at hand
through which the church could be freed, not from its unity, but
from its blind unity." The Reformation, however, is only "a
transition to the third period" when the inner unity will be
realized; this is before us, the Johanine age of Love embracing
all mankind (Ib. 324ff.).

VIII

CONCLUSION

"A gentleman present exhibited a ring, received from England, in the form of a serpent. 'Is the serpent the symbol of English philosophy?' said Schelling to me. 'Oh no!' I answered, 'the English take it to appertain to German philosophy, because it changes its coat every year'—'A proof,' he replied, 'that the English do not look deeper than the coat.' "

(*Diary, Reminiscences and Correspondence of Henry Crabb Robinson*, Vol. 1, p. 83. Boston, 1870.)

In Schelling's mind every subject took a speculative turn. Metaphysician always, the kernel conception of his whole speculation has been the subject of this work. Biographical notes introductory to each chapter reveal the influence of changing circumstances and of new investigations, but always one motive predominates—to systematize all knowledge under one supreme principle. Though the periods of his life have brought different subjects to his attention, and each is marked by a re-coloring of his final principles, it is only the "coat" that changes. Above all finite consciousness and empirical reflection, above the departmental truths of the various natural sciences, above the separation of nature from mind, above the disjunction of freedom and determinism, and, finally, above the diversity of religions stands always the all-embracing One. A study of his Absolute has forced upon us an account of his philosophy that includes reference to every phase of it, and, by attending to the speculative content, we have seen that his Absolutes determine the conjunction of his other conceptions.

His dominating impulse to see the One in All is the secret of those far-reaching influences upon his generation to which we have made brief references in their place. That no future generation has perpetuated his name by attaching it to a system is due to the fact that it was alien to his genius to formulate a system in a preservable whole. Always constructing again from the ground up, but building no abiding place, we have had to follow him from construction to construction, marking only the central conceptions and difficulties in each, and the use of old materials as he re-builds again.

As we now attempt a synoptic view of constructions chronologically developed, the three-fold outline of our conclusion is determined by those elements in which we find a persistent consistency. While this should rescue Schelling from the customary charge of fundamental inconsistency, it also offers considerations of permanent significance to a philosophy of God. These consistent elements are: (1) the impersonality of the Absolute, (2) Intellectual Perception as the only true philosophical method, and (3) the sovereignty of the Absolute Intelligence or Will.

From chapter IV we have had to distinguish the Absolute as a pure original unity from the Absolute as a composite unity. In this "conclusion" we shall use the term "the Absolute" to refer exclusively to the pure original unity, the chief characteristic of which is absolute identity before the beginning of process (which process has sometimes been that of philosophical construction, sometimes that of nature, sometimes that of history). For the composite unity, which is the Absolute ruling the the process, we shall use the expression "the Archetypal Mind" (or "Intelligence" or "Will"), which fairly combines all Schelling's terms and meanings. We may note that even when the Achetypal Mind was Reason, it was as practical reason or Will that it ruled over the process (above pp. 39, 43).

I

In Schelling's use of the term "God," we have to distinguish between his earlier and less guarded application of it, and his later and more guarded. As a general rule it is only when by "God" he is thinking of the Absolute (the pure original unity) that he equates them (in chapters I-V). When, however, he is thinking of the God of religion, or God as a personal Being, he is careful to distinguish God from the Absolute (in chapters VI-VII). Throughout all chapters personality is denied to the Absolute. This fact is especially interesting in face of those expressions in which Schelling appears (even to himself) to be supporting

Christian Theism, for to such a view initial absoluteness would be a most important attribute of the personal God.

When, beginning with the Absolute as I or Will, whose chief philosophical significance is that it is that in which both the form and the content of knowledge unite in one, Schelling says that this alone is God, this God is without object, consciousness, unity of consciousness, personality (above p. 11). When the Absolute becomes Productivity no predicates belong to it (p. 26), except of course, that it is unconscious; to represent it as a personal Being would be a crude misunderstanding of Idealism (p. 27). In the System of Identity, the pure initial identity, the essence of the Universe, is a nocturnal abyss of inactivity (pp. 36, 41). When invited, in religion's name, to recognize God as higher than his Absolute, he refuses to recognize any higher (p. 49). In his Philosophy of Freedom, the Unground has no consciousness or personality (p. 59), and afterwards, when he comes to study the God of the religious consciousness, he becomes aware of the incongruity of using the term "God" for the pure original unity. A° is an unconscious Intelligence (p. 65), and between this absolute Subject and God there is an important distinction (p. 66); the Godhead, as pure Love, is the opposite of personality (p. 69). Finally, the pure original That had better be called Superdivinity or the Godhead's Prius (p. 81). All this shows Schelling's clear insight into the fact that any "God" that may be established as a necessity of thought, as, for instance, by the Ontology that is at the heart of historical Rationalism, is not one for whom the category "personal" is satisfactory (cf. pp. 80, 82). In accordance with the demands of his own method of Intellectual Perception, a personal God must be given up in order to commence philosophical construction (pp. 66, 82).

It is clear from the foregoing that the Absolute which is a presupposition of the experiencing mind is itself no mind. But another Absolute appears (in chapter IV) whose beginnings are as eternal as that of the pure original unity's own. This is the Archetypal Mind (the composite unity) which the Absolute comes to be, or which it is in another aspect. It is this which Schelling, in his later and guarded use of the term, calls "God."

By relating Schelling's conceptions in the only way that is possible to us, we find that his most consistent view of this Archetypal Mind leaves it unconscious. Before being treated in the System of Identity, where it appears as the composite unity of the ideal and the real, and, as such, constitutes Absolute Knowledge (p. 39), it was anticipated in the World-Soul which shaped the world into a system (p. 19), in the absolute Ether which was the ground-type of all products and in which there was an absolute duality (p. 23-4), in the absolute Self-consciousness that was synthetic (p. 29), and in the eternal Unconscious which acted as purpose in nature, as genius in art, and as providence in history (p. 32). Refusing to follow his contemporaries who made teleology presuppose a conscious intention, Schelling made it a constitutive law of the unconscious universal organism. Later, the composite unity becomes the World of Ideas (p. 52), the Absolute Mind (p. 61), or, again, the World-Soul as the union of the irrational Will and the rational understanding (pp. 68, 69); finally, it is the absolute What or the World-Soul as the bond of the three potencies of the Existing, which Existing is the Idea of total possibility, and which, as Soul of the World, is without independent Being (pp. 81, 89).

By relating in this way Schelling's views regarding the Archetypal Mind from the beginning of his works to their completion we recognize a fundamental consistency. But what becomes of his Theism? We have already emphasized the denial of personality to the Absolute, to which we now add that even in his theological speculations he never finds any way of attributing "consciousness" to the Archetypal Mind except in so far as it stands in relation to nature's finite process or to the finite experiencing mind. All his ascriptions of personality to God have to be read in the light of his definitions of personality with which we have taken pains to accompany them. His "Monotheism" is apparently not to be taken very seriously for, after all, self-willed personality is finally to disappear and everything is to end in Pantheism (p. 97).

Very oddly is the term "personality" used when applied to the three potencies to make them the Father, Son and Holy Ghost (p. 92), and, in any case, it seems to escape his attention that it must be derogatory to the Trinity's dignity to have to reckon with the Achetypal Mind or World-Soul standing above the potencies as their bond within the world-process, and with the Absolute or impersonal super-divine That standing as the process's Prius! In spite of Schelling's ambition in making a transition to Theology to do something distinctive for all Germany (p. 57), the historian of Theology is completely silent with respect to his speculations, and contents himself with recording that Schelling's later philosophy "has had no influence upon the development of Theology" (Otto Pfleiderer: *Development of Theology in Germany since Kant*, p. 67).

Since Schelling came to view the task of philosophy as twofold, first to say with apodictic certainty what the Archetypal Mind would be if it were, and then to look to experience for an inductive verification of this, the evidence for a personal God must be sought empirically. History presents us with an impressive tradition of religions whose first thought of a God has been of a "Thou"; persons have sought persons, the heart of man has longed for a Heart that beats like his own (p. 97). This is undeniable. But here two comments must be made. In the first place, Schelling's most consistent view is that the "consciousness" of God is first reached in the Ur-Man's consciousness. In this Ur-Man's consciousness, however, God's consciousness and Man's consciousness are identical in a pure original unity which, like the Absolute, has no consciousness (pp. 64, 73, 93). Then, with regard to the God who has revealed himself in religious history, a history which began with man's fall from that primal unconscious innocence, it can only be the development of the human ideas of God that Schelling presents as a "development of God," and, in agreement with this, a personal God's existence remains to him a "free" conviction (p. 89). In the second place, in his cry for a Person, the language of his heart is at variance with the language of his head, for no loneliness could be lonelier than that in which he insists the philosopher must begin, to whom the Absolute is absolutely impersonal (pp. 66, 82), nor any undertaking more independent of any external aid than his own *a priori* construction of the Archetypal Mind (p. 85).

II

Schelling's general term for the method according to which alone philosophy is possible is Intellectual Perception. To suggest an inner relationship between Kant and Schelling, his Absolute is an apotheosis of the Intellectual Perception which Kant rejected in his Critique of Pure Reason as a mere empty abstraction from the dualism of blind percepts and empty concepts. His Archetypal Mind is an apotheosis of the Intuitive Understanding which absolutist critics of Kant have found him implicitly accepting in his construction of God as the Ideal of Knowledge. That Schelling's foundation principle is "shot out of a pistol" is thus only half true. We will accept this Hegelian criticism with regard to the Absolute; with regard to the Archetypal Mind, however, there is something to be said for Schelling's ill-humored reiterations that he gave Hegel all he knew.

In insisting that there can be no philosophy without Intellectual Perception (p. 38) Schelling is looking upon philosophy as a science which offers apodictic certainty. What Kant in his Ethics took on faith, Schelling will only take by knowledge, and by a knowledge that is absolute. Man, therefore, must possess a faculty by which he becomes one with absolute knowledge, and this faculty is Intellectual Perception. Confining ourselves to those aspects of this faculty to which Schelling always remained true, we observe, firstly, that it is immediate oneness with the Absolute, and, secondly, that it is oneness with the Archetypal Mind also and enables a conscious construction of its principles.

With regard to the first aspect we are almost silenced at once, for words can add little to what is meant by immediate knowledge of the Absolute (p. 49). In this oneness with the Absolute we share the Absolute's pure eternity and bliss (p. 12), but there is no consciousness there, for consciousness requires a duality of subject and object. This immediate vision is purely unconscious (p. 38), a death-like condition in which we share the Absolute's own unconsciousness (p. 66), and it is the agreement of the heart with certain knowledge (p. 71). Such expressions impinge upon mysticism and Schelling accepts the alliance (p. 43). If the expressions disagree it is simply because the completion of all experience would be having no experience left to be experienced and thus the same as not having begun, because, that is, there is no difference between knowing everything and knowing nothing.

So far as Schelling would give reasons for the Absolute, we may note two arguments. In the first place, given any duality, e. g. that between an observer and that which is observed, these two, as part of one system of relations, require a unity prior to their separation or else they could not be related (p. 59). In the second place, the Absolute must be absolutely first else that which preceded it would be, and this would be the Absolute (p. 81); in other words, there cannot be an infinite regress. In so far as Schelling would make the prior unity an unconscious Absolute and not merely another conscious observer, the two arguments are one. A parallel problem to this will reappear presently in connection with the "circularity" of Schelling's system; here we need only mention that, in always putting the unconscious Absolute experienced by Intellectual Perception as his starting point, he takes unconscious infinite being to be a higher state of being for man than a state of being which is conscious of itself as finite being.

With regard to the other aspect of Intellectual Perception, it belongs to the intellect in perceiving the Archetypal Mind in its productive activity, and is the ability to construct its principles and conditions. This, in the first place, is the art of being so identified with nature that we become one with nature's mind. Comparisons here are helpful. Art, for example, is not an imitation of nature; Beauty is the actual (p. 44). The poet is one with the Archetypal Beauty and his Mythology developed as speech developed (p. 44); true art is a completely selfless production (p. 96). Similarly, Truth is the actual. The inspired investigator of nature lives a life in and with nature, expressing the eternal, creative, original Force of the world which produces all things out of itself (p. 44-45); he becomes one with the pure unconscious activity of nature from which the human perceiver is abstracted (p. 38). Similarly, Reason or Will is the actual, and by Intellectual Perception the philosopher embraces the Absolute Reason from which the human reasoner has been ab-

stracted and perceives immediately the movement of the unconscious universal Mind (p. 39), or engages in pure thinking upon
the What of things (p. 96); he is one with the pure productivity
going forth into infinity (p. 27).

This image of artistic and scientific activity assumes that the
less conscious may be the more beautiful and the more true.
The artist and the scientist in becoming one with the higher
beauty and truth are to exercise less and less conscious control;
or, if comparative adverbs are beside the mark, in being one with
the Archetypal Mind they have no conscious control whatever.
Since, however, we ourselves know no higher word for the most
clever of nature's unconscious productivity than "instinct," this
seems to us very much like saying that they become merely
instinctive animals, with an instinct as unerring as genius is
unconscious. As the Psalmist has it: "He giveth his beloved
in sleep."

We may imagine a scientist sitting in his arm-chair engrossed
in that scientific monthly, *The World*, regarding this, meanwhile
as a pursuit which for him is absolutely necessary. Some inborn
instinct of curiosity of which, we shall say, he is for the moment
happily unconscious, compels this perusal, and his mental
activity continues no more reflected upon than in the case of
another who at this same moment knows neither time nor
place in an intensity of absorption in Greek Mythology. We
cannot, however, agree that this fulfills the conditions for any
scientific creativity. The least the scientist can do to display
any touch of inspiration is to release himself from the spell of
absorption in his observation of *The World*, and, looking over
his shoulder, as it were, or as an observer of himself observing,
to look down from this higher reflective viewpoint upon a world
full of observers and their observations. Schelling, however,
in presenting Intellectual Perception as first of all a non-reflective
process, in asking the scientist to look over his own shoulder and
see only the pure observer who is observing nothing, is asking
nothing more than that he fall asleep over his magazine.

This situation is not relieved if we consider the philosopher's
gift of selfconsciousness. Nature as an immature intelligence
(p. 26) reaches selfconsciousness in man; this selfconsciousness

with which we are dealing is an absolute selfconsciousness, and since time is a category of a finite mind, it is primarily outside of all time (p. 30), quite apart from the world of sense-perception. It would thus appear to be a oneness with that "hidden ingenuity" of which Kant spoke, by which the material of sensation is joined to mental representations wholly yonside of the threshold of consciousness. But with reflective selfconsciousness annihilated, instead of being, as we are supposed to be, in the grip of absolute Reason, all our distinctly human rationality is gone. There is here, therefore, no distinction to be made between the Absolute outside of all relations, and the Archetypal Mind, which however, correctly considered, should be in a relation to the finite process that offers a differentiated unity of the principles which are in perfect equilibrium in the Archetypal Mind; we are thus where we were in discussing Intellectual Perception as oneness with the Absolute. We must pass to consider in the second place the conscious construction of the Archetypal Mind offered us by Intellectual Perception.

As the artist's perception, whose genius consists in being one with the eternal Unconscious, becomes objective in a work of art for everyone's sense-perception (p. 33) so the philosopher's gift consists in being able to repeat the unconscious in consciousness (p. 28); he finds in the original, necessary, unconscious activity an inner organism of principles to be investigated with freedom (pp. 28, 85). He descries and constructs the Archetypal Mind, although to do so the finite mind has, of course, arisen. The finite mind is a subject that has the temporal phenomenal world as its object; it has made an artificial separation of opposites which are one in the Archetypal Mind.

Thus, while according to the former aspect perception was unmediated, it is now mediated by the finite; human thinking in copying the divine thinking must lean also upon finite thinking. In other words, the pure infinite intellect cannot be perceived by perceiving simply the pure infinite intellect. In order to know what the two are which are one in the Archetypal Mind the finite world of sense-perception has become an element in the perception of the infinite intelligible world. This is the paradox, if not the condemnation, of Schelling's theory. In abandoning it our only hope for certainty in regard to what is beyond the limits of all possible perception (p. 20) would be an insight into that Mind which is sufficiently sovereign over its subject intelligences that it prescribes for them the conditions to which any theory with respect to the operation of forces beyond the limits of scientific observation must conform.

Since Intellectual Perception is the matrix of the Archetypal Mind, although in each successive period the principles constituting this mind have changed their skin, it ought to be possible to find here some elements common to all the deductions which show the mark of their common origin. It is likened to Plato's transcendental memory (p. 85). This remembering is not remembering in the strict sense of the term as we apply it to the recollection of what has previously been in consciousness, but it is bringing into consciousness the intellectual functionings that have been going on unreflected upon; it is a reproduction of what was produced pre- or non-consciously. Intellectual Perception is also an inner dialogue (ib.). Conscious reflection puts its questions to the infinite unconscious productivity. Here human thinking is, by its very nature, a force which retards or limits the unconscious infinity, this latter being an expansive or unlimited force. Then human thinking wants to expand itself beyond the limits it has introduced, that is, it wants to win back its all-embracing pre-conscious infinity (cf. pp. 29, 32). By this account of the matter the philosopher has reconstructed the dialectic movement of thesis, antithesis and synthesis which takes place in the mind unconsciously or mechanically (p. 28).

Also in that simple *schema* we have in embryo the two principles of the Archetypal Mind. The first principle is most often defined by the same term that is used for the Absolute itself, but now, in the Absolute Duality, it is in relation to a second principle, this second principle being an activity which prescribes limits to the first. Again, since the finite phenomenal world has arisen, and in this the two principles are at strife, the whole movement of the finite is towards the Absolute which the Archetypal Mind becomes again when it no longer has the finite world set over against it. There is thus also throughout

Schelling's work the Absolute set at the end of an infinite task. The proof for God is progressive, and only when the finite's end is reached, can the proof for God be completed (pp. 32, 71, 95). What demonstration will then be offered will be a restoration of the immediate Intellectual Intuition for which the finite world no longer exists. A system is complete when it returns to its starting point (p. 27-8).

III

Upon that jovial evening at Jena when Schelling asked if the serpent was the symbol of English philosophy, the play of wits fell around what will ever remain the most fitting symbol of Schelling's own philosophy—a ring in the form of a serpent. This is better than our other suggestion of a graph that reaches from zero x to zero y. The Absolute with which it starts is a Will which is in such complete equipoise that it neither wills nor does not will (p. 65). The Archetypal Mind with the potencies of this Will in tension is the Universe which is God's Irony (p. 86). The finite phenomenal world is man's deception (p. 95), and amid the great unrest of life, the Will that wills nothing is the true goal (p. 73). Thus Schelling finds a charm in the lines:

"Die zarte Gottheit ist das Nichts und Uebernichts,
    Wer Nichts in allem sieht, Mensch, glaube, dieser sieht's."

(*W. I, 8, 234.*)

The mood is medieval. A Transition to a positive philosophy revealed the demand of the heart for better things and called the bliss of this nothingness only a negative blessedness (above p. 96). To the modern mood, as we see it in contrast to the medieval, this circle is, however, unmitigated wretchedness. As Foss expresses it at the close of "The Higher Catechism":

"The very farthest star
But rims a sea of other stars that stretches just as far.
There's no beginning and no end. As in the ages gone,
The greatest joy of joys shall be the joy of going on."

It is not that there is anything wrong with Idealism, but it is when we qualify our Idealism by the term Absolute that an unanswerable difficulty arises. How deep this difficulty is and how it persisted throughout Schelling's philosophy we have adequately shown (pp. 87-88), and with this we may compare Schelling's own criticism of Hegel (pp. 77-78.)

Taking its central concept to be selfconsciousness there was no way to get to an absolute selfconsciousness, or a selfconsciousness from which the consciousness of the not-self is excluded; or beginning with an absolute selfconsciousness there was no way to get to the consciousness of the not-self. Taking Intellectual Perception as its method, with the affirmation that here we do get to an absolute selfconsciousness, there is then no way from this unconscious to consciousness; there was no way in which Intellectual Perception could mean anything apart from sense-perception, and yet it would perceive the intellect without the senses. All would be well for its logic if the finite phenomenal world were utterly denied, but it is not. Nor can it be for the Archetypal Mind must depend upon the finite mind. As simply an Absolute, God would be only *Deus implicitus* (p. 65); if no quantitative difference is set up the Archetypal Mind would not be actual (p. 42); the composite unity needs the differentiated unity in order to reveal itself and to persist (pp. 24, 30, 35, 39, 68); without a living Realism, Idealism would be a disembodied spirit (p. 59).

Instead of clearing up this problem, Schelling's Positive Philosophy simply emphasizes it. We have presented its task as three-fold (pp. 86, 93, 95). Its first two aspects are directly concerned with the task of getting the finite out of the infinite. This is accomplished by taking that which is the ideal goal of the finite process and making it so Lord of the process that it is absolute Freedom to set it up or not to (p. 89); the absolute Personality whom we found earlier as the God who was the final goal (p. 64), we now find as the absolute Personality which is able to begin everything (p. 92). Or, analogously, the Ur-Man because he is absolutely free, is able to act egoistically and commit the sin that needs all the aeons of time to expiate (p. 94; cf, 28, 64, 73). The essence of this solution is the assumption that the absolutely free can do anything. The fact of the matter is, as Schelling himself has always recognized, that the production of any finite product involves limitation; in other words, that the absolutely free can do nothing at all.

It is difficult for us to see that anything is lost except a serpent-like ring if we accept the "absolute" as an infinite goal only. The disciples of Schelling among the scientists may have been one with an Archetypal Mind, but when we enquire into the nature of the Mind with which any "inspired investigator" must be one, we need not represent it as an absolute beyond the reach of philosophical reflection. It is only when the scientist looks over his own shoulder and sees himself and all other observers making observations that he can form his hypotheses and paint his world-picture. Like a creative artist he may formulate laws in response to some instinctive feeling that he never stops to question. After plotting the isolated dots that register his actual observations, he may join the dots with a curve simply because a curve is prettier than the isolated dots it joins, and, like the artist (p. 32), have a feeling of "infinite satisfaction" in the "infinite harmony" he has wrought. But this does not mean either that his instinct is unerring or that the work of his creative imagination need not come before the bar of conscious reflection. Perhaps it is too much to ask that he see *all* that he is doing in constructing his world-image, but the least—and the most— a true philosopher can do is to look over the scientist's shoulder and see him constructing this image. It is thus that he may come by the "principles of possibility" without which the scientist cannot "put a question to nature" (p. 23), without which, then, as Schelling would insist, there can be no science.

Let us suppose that it is the Theory of Relativity our inspired investigator is formulating. The philosopher sees that in any formulation of its principle the scientist uses the words "independent of the relative." The philosopher cannot but be interested in the motive this implies for he can think of no better definition of ultimate truth than that which is "independent of the relative," unless, with some dissatisfaction with the negative term "independent" he make the statement positive and define the end of all his seeking as that which, when found, would be "inclusive of the absolute" or would represent an actualized totality of all possible points of view. Though he knows well that this ultimate truth is attainable in no finite time he can at least appeal for truth to that Archetypal Intelligence that represents a completion of all knowledge that is to be acquired in finite experience, and can measure his knowledge of today by an approximation to it. Thus our Relativist, in seeking a point of view that is "independent of the relative," has, as his *a priori*, just such an Intelligence; in finding that his science is best served by such a point of view he is recognizing that it serves his purpose best to copy it; and in affirming that the laws of Physics are true when so formulated, has expressed his conviction that ultimate truth is in its keeping.

But it may be said that a point of view that is "independent of the relative" is an expression of what the scientist *wants* and not an expression of what he has. In fact, so much does science want this that there could be no science at all if each observer were left to the particular point of view which is only his own. To an older generation of scientists it might have seemed supererogatory to formulate a theory that made a point of saying what any observer truly observed must be true for all observers. Since they always took for granted that nature was uniform, why make a theory of it? As the philosopher sees the scientist doing this he sees him formulating and accepting that which has been at the foundation of all science. He sees him demanding of himself what has, in fact, never been observed by any scientist, nor can be, namely, that the point of view of any observer be independent of his relative point of view; and if this demand is true, if it is a demand that *ought* to be made, then in making it the scientist is now copying a universal Archetypal Will.

We shall see presently that Schelling, in his last deduction of the Archetypal Mind put Intelligence and Will together. Our brief glance at a relatively recent scientific theory shows how a similar result is possible simply by watching the scientist at work. And if they are to be put together in the right way it would appear that Will comes first. The formula was wanted by the scientist and the formula that was wanted was a formula that viewed reality *sub specie aeternitatis*. We have recognized that the Archetypal Intelligence was an ideal to which finite experience could only progressively approximate; we may now add that no will has a right to be called sovereign which makes an approach to the ideal impossible. As negations of this Archetypal Will we have Descartes' "pineal gland" at the beginning of modern speculative science and Eddington's "quantum action" as one of its most recent contributions. Pseudo-science, with the pseudo-theology that prompts or welcomes it, in trying to make a gap of indeterminacy or unknowability to be filled up by God, is worthy of all the contempt Schelling would heap upon it. What it is really doing is to make a chasm through which we fall into an abyss of skepticism.

If Schelling had viewed the goal of the finite process as unattainable, he would have left us with the joy of going on, and instead of a "ring" we should have had a progress. Whether he regarded the goal as attainable in a finite time it is difficult to say. The "infiniteness" of the finite process has been a thought often with him. A tendency dwells in the finite to lose itself in the infinite, but since this is eternally impossible, he believes in immortality (p. 13-4); and, again, the absolute point of equilibrium of the organizing intelligence may lie in infinity (p. 30). In our science we can only approximate infinitely to the real (p. 19) and such approximation is at the same time the pursuit of a common ideal, and, with ever new unknowns to be conquered by ever increasing knowledge, this approach to the real-ideal is an infinite task (p. 25-6). To these references from his Transcendental Philosophy and his Philosophy of Nature we could add others from his Philosophy of History, which, while regularly envisaging the goal as attainable, do so in a poetic strain and refrain from ever asserting that it is attainable in a finite time (pp. 31, 55, 64, 73, 97; cf. 96). He cannot have it both ways, and having relieved his system of its circularity, we accept the suggestion in his use of terms that is inconsistent with his main viewpoint, and take a view of the goal that leaves us with a progress that is dynamic. Adam, having regained his paradise in the New Jerusalem, has sufficient finiteness left to help himself to its monthly fruits.

Again, Schelling's insistence upon an Absolute with which to begin, when not appealing *ad hominem* to a non-reflective Intellectual Perception, amounts to an objection to an infinite regress (p. 105). The insistence caused the unanswered and unanswerable question. Having saved for ourselves the prospect of an infinite approach to an unattainable ideal we turn again to the starting point and what was Schelling's unanswerable problem now is, How comes the philosopher to assume that reflective viewpoint that enables him to look over the scientist's shoulder and observe his recorded ideas or the implications of the activity which to the scientist himself may be simply instinctive? Since Schelling's unanswerable question was through denying that this was simply a reflective viewpoint, the problem is gone in affirming that it is. That is all that need be said. But to resolve the matter beyond further discussion, we would affirm that the problem of the beginning of any consciousness whatsoever is equally an infinite task for observation and reflection as is the approach in consciousness towards the infinite ideal; it is the failure on the part of contemporary Psychology to recognize this that has caused so much confusion in its accounts of the "immediate datum."

It is interesting in this connection, especially in view of the fact that Schelling usually applies the terms used for his Absolute to the first principle of the Absolute Mind, to observe in his later definitions of the first principle expressions that fit in ill with the insistence elsewhere upon an absolute origin. The first principle is a vague longing (p. 60), somewhat like the semi-conscious condition of dreaming, which contains the possibility of an intelligence it has not yet become (p. 67), and, finally, the possibility of beginning is smoothed out by a $\mu\grave{\eta}$ $\check{o}\nu$ which is not an $o\hat{v}\kappa$ $\check{o}\nu$ (pp. 82, 86; cf. 94).

The constant return of his mind to this problem forces the comment that "the light that shone upon him in 1801" came from a sun that was setting in the east. Better to have stood by the significance of a philosophic mind which was a higher reflective mind and whose existence was never doubted than to have invented the unanswerable conundrum its alternative turned out to be! But never yielding the absoluteness of the purely Rational Philosophy he placed a Positive Philosophy beside it which demanded an appeal to experience to confirm the deductions of the former (p. 76). Had he regarded the former as less "necessary" and the latter as less "free," had he permitted the latter to modify the former, the jest at his expense that goes round the students at Jena today, which says that he postponed his first lecture on the Philosophy of Nature until he had found some empirical data to fill it out, would never have been invented, and the result would have been an Idealistic Empiricism such as is offered us in our own day by Professor Singer (*Mind as Behavior and Studies in Empirical Idealism*. Columbus, 1924).

A critical glance at Schelling's final definition of God will show its significance, hidden to this day. We expressed this simply as *Deus = existentia essentiae + essentia existentiae* (p. 84), Schelling's thought being that God is the free existence of that which he is necessarily conceived to be. Whether God so conceived actually existed depended upon an appeal to history, and, as we have shown, it was not established with certainty (p. 103). We have therefore only to consider how God must be conceived, and for this we have a final analysis of the Archetypal Mind (the "Existing").

Schelling regarded Kant's teaching with regard to the Ideal of Pure Reason as that to which all later philosophical development must attach itself (W. II, 1, 183), and his own analysis supplements it. As a general expression to designate the Archetypal Mind he uses the phrase "the infinite potency of knowledge" which is "the infinite potency of existence" (p. 81-2). Since here "potency" connotes both possibility and power, he is presenting a view of what would be at once an infinite Intelligence and an infinite Will. Than this we can conceive of no better philosophical definition for God; it was just such a definition that our reflection upon science suggested.

The detailed analysis of the Archetypal Mind into three potencies reminds us of Kant's Categories of Modality. The movement is from bare possibility (pure "ability to be") and pure actuality ("the pure existing") to the union of the two in a picture of actualized possibility (p. 82-3). Together they constitute the vision of the actualization of the "Idea of total possibility" in the sense of an actualization of all possible points of view in a single point of view. Again, this movement is primarily a movement of Will, the will that can do anything if it acquires the knowledge which is its power. The union of the possible "quiescent" and the actual "pure will" (ib.) is the vision of the "Idea of total possibility" in the sense of an actualization of the infinite power of knowledge. This Archetypal Mind, which is at once Intelligence and Will, is the Soul of the World in so far as all things in themselves express the whole (p. 89). The Archetypal Mind is beyond good and evil, but the goodness of each finite mind consists in expressing the Soul of the whole.

The Archetypal Mind, thus analyzed into Knowledge and Will, is "the conception of all conceptions" (p. 84). In abandoning his earlier Ontology it would seem that Schelling's word "Idea" really means "Ideal," and that "the conception of all conceptions" is really "the ideal of all ideals." Yet we must grant it whatever present actuality is emphasized when in writing of the "goal" Schelling underlines the words, "it has been thought." "Therefore there is nothing more to be thought *beyond* this existence, therefore also it is no longer to be doubted, it is the absolutely undoubted existence." "If we come by it thinking is completed and finds its complete satisfaction" (p. 86).

BIBLIOGRAPHY

Supplementary to Joh. Jost's *F. W. J. von Schelling, Bibliographie der Schriften von ihm und über ihn. (Bonn) 1927.*

I. *Complete Works*

(1-14) —Schellings Werke. Nach der Originalausgebe in neuer Anordnung herausgegeben von M. Schröter. (München) 1927-8. (Six volumes. Six still to appear.)

(13-14)—Philosophie der Openbarung. Vertaalt in het Nederlandsch door A van der Linde. (Amsterdam) 1862.

III. *Separate Writings*

(32)—The Practical Effects of Modern Philosophy. A short extract from Schelling's "On the Ego as the Principle of Philosophy, or On the Unconditioned in Human Knowledge." Translated by Chas. L. Bernays. *Journal of Speculative Philosophy,* Vol. 3, p. 190, 1869.

(36)—Introduction to the Philosophy of Nature. Extract translated by T. Davidson. *Journal of Speculative Philosophy,* Vol. 1, pp. 193-220, 1867.

(37)—Introduction to Idealism. Extract translated by T. Davidson. *Journal of Speculative Philosophy,* Vol. 1, pp. 159-165, 1867. Reprinted in D. S. Robinson's *Anthology of Modern Philosophy,* p. 564. (New York) 1931. Transcendental Idealism. Selections. Benjamin Rand's *Modern Classical Philosophers,* p. 535. (Boston) 1924.

(39)—Bruno. Mit Einleitung und Registern neu herausgegeben von Christian Herrmann. (Leipzig) 1928.

(40)—On the Method of University Study. Translated by Ella S. Morgan. *Journal of Speculative Philosophy,* Vols. 11 (p. 92) to 15, 1877-81. Selection reprinted in Robinson's *Anthology.*

(44)—The Philosophy of Art. Oration on the Relation Between the Plastic Arts and Nature. Translated by A. Johnson. (London) 1845. (Jost, p. 7, No. 5.)

(53)—Recherches philosophiques sur l'essence de la liberté humaine. Traduction de Georges Politzer. (Paris) 1926.

V. *Appearing in Periodicals*

(63, II)—Esposizione del mio sistema filosofico. Traduzione, introduzione e nota a cura di Ettore de Ferre. (Bari) 1923.

VII. *Schelling's Correspondence*

1911—Aus Schellings Nachlass. Neue Briefe. Herausgegeben von Otto Braun.

VIII. *Books and Articles Upon Schelling*

1800—C. G. Schütz. Vertheidigung gegen Schellings sehr unlautere Erläuterungen über die Allgemeine Lit. Zeitung. (Jena).

1812—Schaffroth. Blicke auf die Schellingisch-Jacobi'sche Streitsache. (Stuttgart.)

1942—E. Zeller and Wilhelm Vatke. Berichte über Schellings neues System. Theologische Jahrbücher, p. 413; p. 606.

1845—J. A. Seubert. Ob Schelling? Ob Schmitt? Oder Dr. Schelling's und Dr. Schmitt's Offenbarungsphilosophie. (Mainz).

1847—J. J. Tengstrom. Evolutionem principii, quo superstructa est speculatio philosophica, ab Anselmo Cantuariensi usque ad Schellingium progrediens, adumbrandi periculum. (Helsingforsiae).

1850—Franz Hoffmann. Baader in seinem Verhältniss zu Hegel und Schelling. Besonderer Abdruck der Vorrede zu Franz Baader's Kleinen Schriften. (Leipzig).

1855—August Böckh. Schellings Verhältniss zu Leibnitz. Bericht über der Verhandlungen der Königl. Preuss. Akademie der Wissenschaften. p. 524, (Berlin). Reprinted, 1859, in Kleine Schriften, Vol. II (Leipzig), Nikolaos Kotzias. Ξχελλίγγιος ἤτοι ὀλιγά τινα περὶ τοῦ βιοῦ καὶ τῆς φιλοσοφίας αὐτου. ('Αθήναις).

1856—Sven Sandberg. Några anteckninger om Schellings philosophi. (Lund).

1860—J. A. Dorner. Ueber Schellings neues System, besonders seine Potenzenlehre. *Jahrbücher für deutsche Theologie*, Vol. 5, p. 101.

J. Hamberger. Schelling und Baader. *Jahrbücher für deutsche Theologie*, Vol. 5, p. 542.

C. Heyder. Schellings Lehre mit bes. Berücksichtigung ihres religionsphilosophischen Inhalts. Abdruck aus *Herzog's Theologischer Real-Encyklopädie*.

1862—Hamberger. Schelling's Philosophie der Mythologie und der Offenbarung. *Deutsche Vierteljahrsschrift für engl.-deutsche Theolog. Forschungen und Kritik.*

Schmidt. Der Neu-Schellingianism. *Der Gedanke*, Vol. II, p. 194.

1863—Eggel. Schelling's Philosophie der Offenbarung nach ihren Grundzügen. *Theologische Studien und Kritiken*, p. 40.

1866—G. V. Lyng. Studier over Schelling. (Christiania).

1867—J. H. Stirling. De Quincey and Coleridge upon Kant. *Fortnightly Review*, new series, II.

1870—Karl Kalich. Cantii, Schellingii, Fichtii de Filio Divinio Sententiam. (Lipsiae).

1872—A. Richter. *Zeitschrift für Philosophie*, Vol. 60, p. 239; Vol. 61, p. 105.

1875—Th. Hoppe. Die Philosophie Schellings und ihr Verhältniss zum Christenthum. (Rostock).

1882—H. Heussler. Schellings Entwicklungslehre. (Besonderer Abdruck aus den *Rheinischen Blättern für Erziehung und Unterricht.*)

1882—Jn. Watson. Schelling's Transcendental Idealism. (Chicago).

1885—J. H. Stirling. Schelling's Poem on England. *Journal of Speculative Philosophy*, Vol. 19, p.103.

1889——Resa von Schirnhofer. Vergleich zwischen den Lehren Schelling's und Spinoza's. (Zürich).

Cecily (Ullman) Sidgwick. Caroline Schlegel and her Friends. (London).

1905—A. S. Dewing. Negation and Intuition in the Philosophy of Schelling. *Harvard Thesis* (unpublished).

Xavier Leon. Fichte contra Schelling. *Comptes rendus du deux. Congrès intern. de philos.*, Geneva.

1906—Erwin Kircher. Philosophie der Romantik. (Jena).

Gust. Meyer. Das Verhältniss der Entwicklungstheorie in Schellings Naturphilosphie zum Darwinismus. (Görlitzer Realgymnasium).

1908—Hans Dreyer. Der Begriff Geist in der deutschen Philosophie von Kant bis Hegel. (Berlin).

Wilhelm Miessner. Schelling, ein Goethephilosoph. *Die Gegenwart*, pp. 150-3.

1909—Franz Schultz. Der Verfasser der Nachwachen von Bonaventura, Untersuchungen zur deutschen Romantik. (Berlin).

W. Greiner. Das Problem der menschlichen Willensfreiheit bei Kant und Schelling. (Jahres-Bericht des Grossherzoglichen Realgymnasium zu Eisenbach.)

A. Faggi. Schelling e la filosofia dell' arte. (Modena).

1910—G. Bolland. Schelling, Hegel, Fechner en de nieuwere theosophie; eene geschiedkundige voor- en inlichting. (Leiden).

Wilhelm Metzger. Schelling und die biologischen Grundprobleme. (Leipzig).

1912—Edmondo Solmi. Il sistema dell' identita di Schelling esaminato de Vincenzo Gioberti. (Torino).

Konr. Müller. Schellings Beziehungen zur alttestamentlichen Wissenschaft. (Breslau).

1913—Carl Siegel. Geschichte der deutscher Naturphilosophie. (Leipzig).

1914—Michele Losacco. Schelling. (Milano).

Fritz. Medicus. Fichtes Leben. (Verhältnis Fichtes zu Schelling und zur Naturphilosophie). (Leipzig).

Otto Braun. Die Schelling-Forschung der Gegenwart. *Die Geistes-wissenschaften*, No. 37, p. 1018.

1917—Franz Rosenzweig. Das älteste Systemprogram des deutschen Ideal-ismus. Ein handschriftlicher Fund. *Sitzungberichte der Heidelberger Aka-damie des Wissenschaften.*

1919—Barbara Allason. Caroline Schlegel; studio sul romanticismo tedesco. (Bari).

1921—Wilhelm Dilthey. Fortentwicklung von der absoluten Vernunft zur Gottpersönlichkeit, dem Willen als Grund der Welt und der Anerken-nung des Irrationalen und Gesichtlichen. *Gesämmelten Schriften*, Vol. IV. (Leipzig).

1921-4—Richard Kroner. Von Kant zu Hegel. (Tübingen.)

1923—Hugo Falkenheim. Neuere Schelling-Literatur. (Supplement to fourth edition of Schellings Leben, Werke und Lehre, by Kuno Fischer.)

1925—Ettore de Ferri. La filosofia dell' identità di Schelling fino al 1802 e suoi rapport stoici. (Torino.)

Frank Rümelin. Schellings Naturphilosophie in ihren Wirkung auf die liberale Staatslehre. (Giessen.)

1926—Paul Genths. Die Identitätsphilosophie Schellings in ihrem Verhältnis zur Religion. (Würzburg.)

J. D. Choudhurv. Das Unendlichkeitsproblem in Schellings Philoso-phie. (Berlin.)

Margaret Adam. Die intellektuelle Anschauung bei Schelling in ihrem Verhältnis zur Methode der Intuition bei Bergson. (Patschkau.)

Toni Rothmund. Caroline Schlegel. (Leipzig.)

1927—Adolf Allwohn. Der Mythos bei Schelling. *Kant-Studien*, 61.

G. J. Dekker. Schellings letzte Wandlung. (München.)

Kurt Leese. Von Jakob Böhme zu Schelling. (Erfurt.)

1928—O. Platenius. Schellings Fortführung der Lehre Kants von Bösen. (Hilchenbach.)

1929—Franz Donay. Der Einheitspunkt in Schellings Philosophie. (Koblenz.)

Joh. Jost. Die Bedeutung der Weltseele in der Schelling'schen Philoso-phie im Vergleich mit der Platonischen Lehre. (Bonn.)

H. Knittermeyer. Schelling und die Romantische Schule. (Mün-chen.)

J. R. Richter. "Intuition" und "Intellektuelle Anschauung" bei Schelling und Bergson. (Ohlau.)

Gustav Osthus. G. H. Schuberts philosophische Anfänge unter besonderer Berücksichtigung von Schellings Einfluss. (Leipzig.)

1931—Hermann Zeitner. Schellings philosophische Idee and das Identität-system. *Beiträge zur Philosophie*, 20. (Heidelberg.)